Jane T. Stoddart

A Letter to G. G.

Jane T. Stoddart

A Letter to G. G.

ISBN/EAN: 9783337956547

Printed in Europe, USA, Canada, Australia, Japan

Cover: Foto ©Andreas Hilbeck / pixelio.de

More available books at **www.hansebooks.com**

A

LETTER

TO

G. G.

Stiff in Opinions, always in the wrong.

LONDON:

Printed for J. WILLIAMS, at No. 38. next the
Mitre Tavern, in Fleet-Street.
MDCCLXVII.

S I R,

Y O U will be furprized perhaps at the receipt of a letter, after fo long an a-lienation of connections. You muft place it to the idlenefs of the country, and to the wantonnefs of holiday time, as I certainly have given up the rights of old acquaintance, and am not interefted to queftion you for your late publications. Indeed every man is *now* at liberty to print what he thinks proper. You may come forth (if you like it) in a tye and in quarto, while your fecretaries appear with bags and in octavo. And you may put what price you pleafe upon your feveral exhi-bitions ; three and fixpence, three fhillings, two fhillings, or even one fhilling. No body is obliged to pay that does not choofe it. The whole is very fair.

If you find any entertainment in note tak-ing, commenting and writing for the pub-

B   lic

lic, when you cannot talk to them, I do not begrudge your employment, and I fee no harm in it. For, altho' one be frequently obliged to bear with a fpeech of three hours, on a thimble full of matter, yet no body is under a neceffity of undergoing the perufal of the fame thing in print.

It has been, however, my misfortune to be at the villa of a friend, during this fhort recefs, where nothing but news papers, pamphlets or cards can be had for the amufement of a bad day and long evenings. By which means I have read three or four late pamphlets, that I fhould otherwife never have looked into, and now (as I underftand they all came from you or your penmen) I fhall by way of revenge (to ufe a card playing expreffion) as well as to fill up the remainder of my time, fend you fome animadverfions in a loofe, epiftolary way, with little method, and with all the freedom of political colloquy. My ftyle, perhaps, you will not relifh; but I do not think you ought to wonder at it, for few men can endure repeated perfeverance in exploded errors and much dull abufe, without rifing up indignant at laft, and being petulant in return. And yet I thought I had reined myfelf in as ftrongly as I could, knowing how provokingly long, and unfatisfactory you would be, that is, how very like the late unfortunate harveft, plentiful in ftraw, but light in the ear. Nay, I knew you well enough to guefs where the envy and the fretfulnefs of your temper would

would lead you. Neverthelefs, I could not have conceived you would have touched fome of the matters you have. Surely the appetite of the public or your own intereft, could never be fufficiently confidered at the time, with the affiftances you are faid to command ; fome better topics might have been found out. Your finecure Newfoundland fecretary might bring the political tittle-tattle or gleanings of coffee-houfes to your ear, whilft your treafury fecretary was hunting out appofite paffages in hiftory, or claffical ornaments in antient authors. At night, the occurrences of both might be fubmitted to your revifion, and thence you might afterwards indite fomewhat that was palatable and fit for your private fecretary to fair copy for the town.

But here I fhould inform you, that many people fhrewdly fufpect the brain of one of your helpmates (the *German* confiderer) to be fomewhat affected, and therefore you fhould examine a little into the matter, before you rely very much upon his pen. Perhaps he is only overloaded with vanity (as might very well happen to a Blackwell-hall factor) from accidental repute as a writer. But it is certain, that the little bufy animal is of late years become wonderfully pert and impertinent. Now (what is very odd) between you and me, many people conjecture, with refpect to his memorable production, that he was no more the genuine father, than old *Colley Cibber* is faid to have been of the *Eafy Hufband,* and for the fame reafon ; namely, the utter

un-

unlikenefs of all the reft of his known and
avowed progeny. In truth, I have heard
that in his political trade he fet out as a de-
pendent on the retainers to a famous old lawyer, (who you may remember) was long
the head-piece of a rotten junto, that con-
ftantly endeavoured in private to depreciate
the eminent fervices of the great minifter
they were publicly acting with, and therefore
clandeftinely retailed to proper emiffaries whatever might contribute to fo honeft, laudable
and national a purpofe. Your run-a-bout
fcribe was much at their heels, and although
he now figures with a fword and bag, was
then but the humbleft of politicians, and dreff-
ed in the plaineft of habits, as became a poor
fimple layman who had but juft quitted the
pulpit and tub. His pen being vacant, and
itching for employ, he put together, as it was
gueffed he would, whatever was purpofely
dropped at proper times, and with convenient
difcretion by thefe retainers to the old lawyer
and junto. This he did (to give him his
due) very well upon the whole, with here
and there *une maudite phrafe pourtant et des
redites ennuyeufes.* But it fo happened, that a
change of the miniftry fell out, before the im-
preffion of his well intended piece could be
finifhed; fo that when it came out, it ferved
quite another fet of men, that in its embryo
were not in view, who inftantly fought out
the editor, and with tranfport careffed and re-
warded him. The good luck of this fcribling
ear-wig was really uncommon; for (if I miftake

take not) the crafty original defigner and fo-
mentor of the factious work would never have
avowed the knowing aught of the matter, and
have only fed the officious writer with kind
gracious looks now and then, and fome cafual
paffing civilities as he fell in his way. However, the vifible favours and open protection
of the new minifters, with an admiffion to
their perfons and tables, being too ftrong for
the head of your friend, quite overpowered
his fmall fenfes, and (what is moft ftrange to
relate) converted at once a fpeaking obfcure
conventicler into a fine gentleman and tory, in
which fphere he has flourifhed ever fince,
noify, petulant and public, and officioufly
exhibiting in the lobbies of either houfe, at
court, in coffee-houfes, and all other places of
common refort, the ftrongeft living example
to be met with of *the great importance of a
man to himfelf*. Therefore before you intruft
him again, implicitly with ftate papers, have
a confultation upon the ftate of his brain.
You may hold it upon *the next* 30th *of January,*
as that is a day I am told concerning which he
has fome particular conceit.

Let me advife you further, and above all
things, as you want popularity yourfelf to a
very unufual degree, to get a popular topic;
and withal to acquire if poffible a right con-
ception of the temper of the times, before you
venture to call upon the public for their regard and attention. It is not induftry or inclination you ftand in need of, for this purpofe,
but a found difcernment. Perfeverance is an

useful quality; but when bestowed on a
wrong scent, only carries a man farther out
of the road, and is really so much sheer ob-
stinacy wholly lost and thrown away. This
you do not seem to be aware of. Besides,
there are certain subjects which you should
never touch upon, such as liberty, property,
America, Spain, Portugal. The very mention of them recalls a long train of ugly ideas,
which are very forbidding in their nature,
and will forever revolt all Englishmen from
you, whilst any notion of a constitution re-
mains, or the smallest idea of national, com-
mercial interest subsists. We wish never
more to hear of the laws of our country being
kept at bay, nay set at defiance, during a
whole administration; nor of our trade with
our colonies being at a stand; nay, exposed
to a civil war for the sake of a pittance of revenue; nor of the inlet of foreign bullion being stopped by new constructions of the letter
of old acts of parliament, on narrow custom-
house ideas, to the irreparable loss of the
whole aggregate state. When a man is desirous of running down others, he should avoid
reminding the world of his own misdeeds.
Things of an heinous nature make a strong
impression whilst they are passing, and are a
long while burying in oblivion. Nay, thanks
to our *annual registers*, they afterward become
objects of reflection in one's study. It is not
long since I read there of a time, when a head-
strong minister for two years together, that is,
during the existence of his administration,
main-

maintained a moft unrelenting warfare, not
only with the trade, but with the laws of his
country; infomuch that mens hearts failed
them for fear, and no judge would venture to
intimate his opinion upon the cleareft of points,
excepting one bold affertor of the liberties of
mankind; until at length a change of minifters took place; and then thofe, who were
prudentially mute and acquiefcent before, became the forwardeft and moft officious in
pronouncing how illegally the wretched miniftry, fo lately difcarded, had acted. Their
terrifying warrant was every where proclaimed
to be no warrant at all, and that there never
was a doubt about the matter. And as I read
on, I found that this very minifter, the inflexible fupporter of the infringement of the
laws of the realm, who would not yield an
inch to them, or the united voice of his coun-
trymen, whilft armed with power, the moment he felt himfelf falling and deferted by
the court (being circumvented and intangled
in fome regency bill, as it was faid) although
avowedly oppofed but by a mere private man,
yielded, gave way; nay, licked the very rod
that corrected him, with all the fubmiffion of
the pooreft, the meaneft and moft fervile of
human creatures. So natural is it for cowar-
dice and tyranny to unite in the fame breaft,
and for obftinacy againft the people to confort
with abfolute refignation to the crown, that is,
fordid felf-intereft to prevail, where the conftitution and patriotifm have made no impref-
fion at all. What a noble champion for liberty

berty muſt ſuch principles make! how popular
with mankind! how happy in himſelf!

A quarto pamphlet on matters of calculation
may do well enough, perhaps, to prove that the
writer has buſied himſelf about figures, is able
to caſt accounts, and may make a diligent and
uſeful firſt clerk or deputy to a money board ;
but will never evince the compiler to have a
genius ſufficient for directing the commerce of
a great trading country, or to be capable of de-
ciding upon the manifold intereſts of a mighty
dominion. Men who are critical about pounds,
ſhillings and pence, are very rarely perſons of
large thoughts, or of very extenſive views.
Their mind is ſo cramped by the detail of common things, and by ſmall attentions, that they
generally neglect objects of more conſequence,
and are in fact what the vulgar very properly
phraſe, but penny wiſe and pound fooliſh.

As chance would have it, I fell firſt upon
two pamphlets about diſpenſing powers, with
mottoes drawn from a late adjudication of a
later ſpeech; I was very averſe from reading
theſe fugitive writings on the primary view
(although I had nothing to do,) being perfectly ſatisfied as an individual, like every body
elſe, both with the embargo and the act of
indemnity. However, as i muſt otherwiſe
have cut in, I even ſet about it. But I now
moſt heartily blame myſelf for my misjudge-
ment, becauſe I ſhould certainly have been
more entertained by any ſort of game, as I
really learned naught from either of the pieces,
but that ſome people at preſent out of place
wεrε

were therefore very angry and had been making much ado about nothing.

Indeed as men of unclear heads when they
attempt to reafon abftrufely, or enter into the
nice diftinctions about principles of government, ufually get out of their depth before
they have done, and talk nonfenfe and mifre-
prefent where they leaft intend it; fo I found
this was the cafe with thefe fcribblers. One
of them for inftance advances that " *falus*
" *populi fuprema lex* fhould be applied to juftifie
" the act, not to authorize the power," and
that the miniftry fhould only have attempted
" to juftifie upon the circumftances." Now, in
a legal fenfe, or in a court of law (to fpeak like
a lawyer) you can *juftify* nothing but what is
authorized by law, and whatever is fo you
may always juftify. If what was done therefore could upon the circumftances be juftified,
the power ordering it muft have had a legal
authority, and confequently no act of indemnity be neceffary; which I prefume neverthelefs was not precifely the meaning of the
pamphleteer, provided he had a glimmering
of what he undertook to write about. For,
an intelligent writer would have faid, that there
was no lawful power exifting, which could
authorize an embargo or prohibition to export,
whilft the act of Charles the IId. was in force
that declared every fuch prohibition to be null;
and therefore the royal proclamation which
did, notwithftanding that ftatute, prohibit exportation, was a violation of the pofitive law
of the land, and confequently neither that, nor

C   what

what was done under it, could be juftified upon principles of law by any means whatever. He might then have ftated (and, if he could, have refuted) the doctrine of a great and extraordinary man, (which I can tell him has many fupporters among the warmeft advocates for liberty;) namely, that the king of this country has ever been invefted with a prerogative during the intervals of parliament to lay embargoes in cafe of famine or other *natural neceffity*, although in no other cafe whatever; that fuch a power muft exift at all times, in all governments, fomewhere, it being effential to the prefervation of a ftate; that in this conftitution, when there is no parliament met, it muft from neceffity be lodged in the executive hand of the government, that is, in the king; that this power can never be mifapplyed, becaufe no man can be deceived about facts like famine, peftilence or fire; that a jury will always be competent judges whether thefe natural neceffities exifted or not; and that the ftatute of Charles IId. never had in contemplation the taking away a prerogative fo effential to the general weal, which derives its force, and an irrefiftable one, from human nature itfelf, and is acknowledged by all the allowed writers upon the laws of nature and nations and the univerfal principles of government; for that this ftatute was aimed only at the prohibitions and licences (which ufed to be formerly granted from time to time on commerical views, as mere political regulations, to particular perfons, ports, and diftricts,)

and

and was enacted on purpofe to eftablifh, upon
larger ideas of trade, a general right of exportation for the future, in every body, and every
place, and at all times; but never was intended to touch or take away from the king, in fuch
great natural emergencies as dearth and famine,
the prerogative of faving his people from
ftarving, by the laying of a fudden embargo on
the neceffaries of life. When your fcribe had
fucceeded fo far, he might have gone on to try
his talents at confounding, mifreporting, and
calumniating the fentiments of another noble
perfon (whofe free fpirit by the bye, whenever
it croffes your way, I perceive makes the very
teeth gnafh in your head, from a well known
caufe.) This bright character he might endeavour to blacken for maintaining that pofitive laws themfelves muft give way, like every
thing elfe, to natural neceffity; for ufing the
words of our law-maxim, *neceffity has no law,*
that is, cannot be bound or reftrained by any,
it implying indeed a contradiction in terms
to fuppofe that it could, becaufe if it could,
it would ceafe to be neceffity. And
where the falvation of the people clear-
ly depends upon the breach of a law of police,
if the minifter at the helm, fhould, notwithftanding, obftinately refufe to tranfgrefs a
ftatute, they would have a right to impeach
him as the caufe of all the detriment that
fhould enfue; *falus populi fuprema lex* being
the primary principle of union in fociety and
the very bafis of all civil government. In
fact, this doctrine has been and muft always

C 2   be

be acted upon in times of real neceffity. It
is true, nevertheless, that the legiflature in
all fuch cafes fhould be affembled, fo foon
as conveniently may be. And this was done
now ; fo that the tyranny (if power exercifed for the good of community may be fo
ftigmatized) or the *lent* of liberty (as this
embargo *to prevent* real *fafting* has been called
by a trope of Hibernian rhetoric) could laft
but 40 days at the utmoft. Such a dreadful
calamity as famine through the land, no-
tified by the addreffes of the feveral corporations, can never be mifunderftood or miftaken.
Whatever is done to ftop it, all mankind
will allow to be well done, to be right and
juft ; every jury and every judge muft do the
fame, and the parliament itfelf, if called upon,
will be obliged by exprefs ftatute to juftify
the fame, not as a favour, but *ex debito juftitiæ*.
I do not contend for any latent prerogative
or *arcanum imperii*, which impowers the
king to fufpend or difpenfe with law; but I
infift that abfolute neceffity does in all cafes
carry its own juftification along with it, becaufe in the nature of the thing it implies a
want of choice, and that nothing elfe could be
done *falva republica*. And by the way too,
upon what principle is it that we have fo un-
animoufly concurred, in declaring it was *right*
his majefty fhould lay the embargo ; all of us
knowing it at the very time to be contrary to
ftatute ; unlefs upon this principle, that the
falus populi required it, which, as the great
primary law of nature making a part of the
law

law of every particular ftate, or political convention of men, is a *fuprema lex*, paramount every pofitive municipal ordinance whatever, and by taking place in the hour of diftrefs, and natural neceffity, fufpends, fuperfedes, difpences with, overturns, and bears down all human regulations before it. In a word, neceffity muft and can only be a law to itfelf. To talk of our conftitution, knowing no fuch principle as the *falus populi*, is to caft the higheft imputation upon it, and to fay it is defective in the neceffary means of falvation, adopted by the univerfe befides. I am fure, if we have no fuch principle in our government, we ought immediately by ftatute to import and incorporate it. But we have it. Befides, where all men agree in an abfolute neceffity of breaking a ftatute, who is to complain of the breach of it? and if fo, where is the call for a fpecial law to indemnify the action? Yes; but may fome *Therfites* fay, there are who do and will complain of the actors; and had they at the time been refifted and killed, I can tell you fuch killing would have been juftifiable in law. Why, then I fay *Therfites*, if there be fuch orators, although I proteft I never heard of any fuch but from you; I have no objection to their having the legiflative indemnity they pray; for my own part, however, I crave no fuch mercy, I am not cowardly enough to intreat or follicit any indemnification whatever. If the reprefentatives of the people find a ftatute to be requifite, they will without queftion bring in a bill for the purpofe. But, as to

thofe

thofe who advifed the meafure, they can only
be profecuted by impeachment; and fhall we
fuppofe that the parliament, who have already approved the proclamation, by addreffing
the king to iffue another for continuing the
very embargo originally laid, will vote for
fuch an impeachment? What a reflection
does the mere fuggeftion carry along with
it!

Some of your friends, however, as I hear,
not content with endeavouring to cavil at and
difparage the words, when they could not
blaft the actions and conduct, of the eloquent
lawyer, alluded to, would fain alfo have found
fault with the language of the great minifter,
his noble friend, as if he had infifted upon the
ftrict legality of the embargo. Infomuch,
that I am told he was obliged to contradict
them by faying in fo many words he thought
the proclamation illegal, and had never called
it legal; but, that he thought it right, notwithftanding, as he perceived every body elfe
did, even the captious gentlemen themfelves,
upon that great fuperintending principle of
all government, the prefervation of the whole.
It was wonderful therefore that heat fhould
arife, when there were only fhades of difference among the deliberants! Efpecially as
Mr. Locke himfelf (that memorable vindicator
of the oppreft rights of mankind, the ableft of
reafoners, and the foremoft of writers upon
civil government and the general principles
even of our conftitution; whofe name, now,
by the pure effect of his arguments, is grown

into

into authority with all free ſtates) : where he conſiders the genuine idea of prerogative, and its true original and ground, abſtracted from the poſitive laws of particular countries, lays it down that " being nothing but a power, in " the hands of the prince, to provide for the " public good, in ſuch caſes, which depend- " ing upon unforeſeen and uncertain occur- " rences, certain and unalterable laws could " not ſafely direct : whatſoever ſhall be done " manifeſtly for the good of the people, and " the eſtabliſhing the government upon its " true foundations, is, and always will be, " juſt prerogative. Whatſoever cannot but " be acknowledged to be of advantage to " the ſociety and people in general, will " always, when done, juſtify itſelf. For the " legiſlators not being able to foreſee and " provide by laws, for all that may be uſeful " to the community, the executor of the laws " having the power in his hands, has by the " common law of nature a right to make uſe " of it for the good of the ſociety, in many " caſes, where the municipal law has given " no direction, till the legiſlative can be con- " veniently aſſembled. Nay, it is fit that the " laws themſelves ſhould in ſome caſes give " way to the executive power, or rather to " this fundamental law of nature and go- " vernment, viz. That as much as may be, " all the members of the ſociety are to be pre- " ſerved, the end of government being the pre- " ſervation of all." The king therefore in the preſent caſe, as having the powers in his hands, was upon the principle of that common law

of

of nature, the good of fociety, advifed by proclamation to prohibit, what the municipal law permitted, until the legiflature could be conveniently affembied ; and this was fummoned to meet much earlier than ufual. The advice is approved. But, it is faid, the parliament might have been fooner affembled. Now I beg leave to infift, it would have been highly incommodious to members, and dangerous in example to have fummoned fuch meeting inftantly, becaufe few could then have attended, and by fuch a precedent (with previous indirect notice to thofe in the fecret) fome future prince might hereafter get any act approved or paffed that he might defire. And therefore it is that Mr. *Locke*, who had revolved fuch exigencies much in his thoughts, very wifely concludes the executive authority muft make ufe of the power in its hands, until the legiflative can be *conveniently* affembled. Where fire, peftilence and famine come upon us, there can be no danger, and there is a propriety, in the exercife of this power. By the bye, the denial of hunger to be a natural neceffity, and the cafting it into the clafs of political neceffities, is fuch an abufe both of words and things, as will never miflead the world, let what logical lawcraftfman foever attempt it. No fophiftry can argue down the feelings of mankind, or make them believe that an embargo for the prevention of famine to the republic, is like the levying of fhip-money for the purfe of the monarch. It amazes me to hear an actual

dearth

dearth denied to be a matter of fact, and treated as the arbitrary conclusion of political reasoning. For, though probable or future scarcity may be the object of speculation and cannot be ascertained, yet present famine is a reality, and must be capable of proof. Men, therefore, are not to be cheated out of their senses, with such fallacies as these, by the cunningest arguer among us. Indeed, had the embargo been issued at the meeting of the first council, when there was merely a scarcity, and but a probability of dearth; it must have been issued upon political speculation and without necessity: and, let me add, had a summons also, for the parliament to meet, then gone forth, it would have frightened and alarmed the public exceedingly, without any sufficient cause. But, when the last council was holden, a famine had begun and stared mankind in the face, the prices of markets and the addresses of corporations concurrently and unquestionably proved the fact; there was, therefore, in that moment, a *natural* call for an immediate embargo, nothing else could answer the exigency of the case, it became indispensibly *necessary*; and the same reason likewise justified, and nothing less would, the convoking of the whole legislature, so *very much* earlier than has been usual, in times of tranquillity, allowing with all due space for distant burgesses (the *Scotch* and the *Cornish*) to assemble.

The embargo, I avow, was contrary to law, but it was layed *pro salute populi*, and

there-

therefore it was juft; for, in cafes of natural neceffity, the good of the people muft be the *fuprema lex*, exprefs yourfelf how you-will, or talk as long as you pleafe about the matter. The parliament are the proper judges of extraordinary acts; they have been called as early as convenience would admit, to judge of the prefent. The embargo has been only extended to the time of their affembling, and now that they are affembled, the whole is fubmitted to their fupreme controul. Every thing has been done with a reference to parliament. We are here for their judgment. Let them give it.

In truth too, I am informed after all, that the principal minifter in the houfe of commons, moved for the indemnity bill himfelf, and befeeched your friends to word it as they liked, for the clearer and more exprefs it was, the more it would fuit his principles; and that thereupon, like true political opponents, they gave up the matter, and left him to do as he thought proper; altercation and not public good, being the whole of their aim. Nay, I hear farther, that meeting you in a large company afterwards, you took occafion, as ufual, to make a very long fpeech upon this very fhort bill, wherein you firft fuppofed many things, and then entered into a long difcuffion of poffible inconvenience and detriment accruing from them; but that fo foon as you had done, the polite minifter fmiled, and faid briefly, truly they were not his ideas, nor thofe of his friends, which you had been com-

combating, but mere chimeras of your own; and *he* therefore *fuppofed* you had given yourfelf fo much agitation merely for amufement and to keep yourfelf in wind; and if fo, he hoped the exercife would do you good ; he was fure what you had faid would do him no harm : and that thereupon, for once in your life, you were laughed into filence. I am perfuaded, my old acquaintance, unlefs you are much altered, you muft have been greatly mortified that you could not raife a difpute.

Now, for my own part, where men have ftruck a bold ftroke to ferve the public, and in fact done what every body declares to be praife-worthy, although out of the pale of the law, I cannot be fcanning every word they may chance to utter. Nay, what we all agree ought to be done by the prince, one can hardly blame any man for faying he had a right to do. And in actual dearths during the interval of parliament, we even hold it the fovereign's duty to fufpend the laws of exportation, convening the houfes however with all due fpeed. Now if this fhould always be done during receffes, feeing no other method can be immediately taken for the relief of the people, it feems to be little more than a difpute, about words, whether the king has or has not a prerogative for fo doing. No body can ferioufly think that liberty can be endangered by fuch a power, limited as it is to the cafe of famine and to the intervals of parliament; becaufe it can never be exerted, but in aid of the fubject, and will not enable a

prince

prince to raife either money or troops to enflave him. I am fure, at leaft, upon fuch an event, it would be very unbecoming a lawyer in high ftation publickly to proclaim to fore-ftallers and cornfactors, that notwithftanding a proclamation, they might legally and by force export, and that if in fo doing they fhould kill thofe who endeavoured to prevent them they might be juftified by law for the deed. For, fuch doctrine can only be flung out with a view to do mifchief, and not out of any re-gard to liberty, or magiftracy; or to the wants of the multitude, or to the order and ftability of government.

Neverthelefs I do not diflike an act of in-demnity, and particularly upon the prefent occafion, as it will remain upon record the ftrongeft poffible teft of the neceffarinefs of parliament to the ratification of every act of ftate, however beneficial and meritorious, however needful; that it is the privilege of *Englifhmen* to be bound only by *exprefs law* and that nothing can be abfolutely valid with-out it. It will demonftrate to pofterity that onr courts of juftice are to liften to nothing but pofitive law; that general arguments of juft and good, the virtue of the beft of princes, the wifdom and reputation of the moft approv-ed minifter, the authority of an unanimous privy council, the applaufe of all ranks of men, the prayers of the multitude, the horrors of natural calamity, the voice of human nature itfelf, I might fay, the vifitation of the Al-mighty,

mighty, are to have no influence on an *English* judge when delivering the law of the land.

Upon reflection too, I can easily conceive a positive written law will be more obvious to the capacities of ordinary men than the general principle of *natural necessity*; and what is still of more consequence, be less liable to the perversions of crafty and designing statesmen. And yet, I believe most men will admit, that plague, famine, and fire are attended with such strong outlines, as not to be easily confounded with the pretended political necessities of ministers however refined by supple and qualifying lawyers. Nevertheless, as there have been men of this last description who have lent their consciences and their arts to uphold and to justify *on the cirumstances of* the case, (that is, on the practice of political offices,) the most flagrant, cruel and unnecessary breaches of the law in violation of personal liberty; and as there have been others of a superior sphere, who have striven to prove actual want and famine to be a political and not a natural necessity: so there may hereafter arise again gowns-men of aristocratical principles and birth, who may at a pinch be ready to maintain any state expedients of the day to be natural and not political necessities. For these reasons, and not for the sake of the present harmless occasion, I shall cherish this retrospective statute that commends and countenances, as well as indemnifies the public-spirited transaction which hath furnished the whole of this discourse.

The

The attempt to abufe any miniftry for pre-
venting a famine, in fpight of a ftatute, is really
(as one of your own friends humoroufly confefied)
much like the impeachment of Gulliver for
extinguifhing a fire in Lilliput palace, by doing what was contrary to law. Mens heads
muft be wrong before they think of gaining
popularity by fuch accufations. I muft
therefore once more repeat, that the faving a nation, notwithftanding a contrariant
act of parliament, is not, nor ever will be a
crime in the eyes of the people. Dear G—,
it is not like a minifter's breaking the law to
arreft and imprifon one of their reprefentatives,
to feize all his private papers, and to ftrip him
of parliamentary privilege, upon the mere fuf-
picion of printing a libel. Upon my word it is
not like locking up a man's perfon in jail, and debarring him pen, ink, paper and friends, upon no
other ground than that of the attorney general's
having called him a libeller, for lafhing an
odious miniftry. There is no natural neceffity
for the difpenfing with law in order to do thefe
things, in any country, at any time; they are
mere political feats and atchievements, or (if
you like the term better) ftate-neceffities, that
is, the mere creatures of wilful, ignorant,
wounded ftatefmen. Any man that runs will
fee the difference. In fhort, you fhould learn
to diftinguifh between things before you throw
away much time in talking about them. What is
done for the falvation of the public, is not like
what is done for the ruin and oppreffion
of individuals. Abufe in words, whether
from

from the mouth or pen, upon three or four miniſters, is not a national calamity like the want of bread, the world can go on notwithſtanding; nor is it a fact ſo readily aſſented to, or ſo eaſily proved. Mens feelings do not co-operate univerſally in the one caſe as in the other. There is not the ſame human ſympathy. Therefore when I hear men calumniating miniſters for ſuſpending laws in order to do good to mankind, as if they had ſuſpended them for the purpoſe of revenging perſonal quarrels in a manner not permitted by law; and recollect that thoſe who labor to raiſe the outcry were the very actors of ſuch enormities, I proteſt it only aggravates the badneſs of their public characters, and makes one more eaſily give credit to the worſt that ever was ſaid of them. And, take it from me, G——, the white-livered envy of a ſunk miniſter, pining after the emoluments of office, will never produce any formidable oppoſition. Nay, I am inclined to think, that the ſickly ſpirit of jealouſy, however it may put on for a moment an uncomfortable ſmile, is only a torment to itſelf; for, by militating with equal fury and rancor againſt good and bad, againſt all that is propoſed of every kind, it ſhews its own unhappy temper, defeats its purpoſe, and revolts every beholder.

In reality, there is as much apparent principle in ſuch conduct, as there is of truth in a man that, after having got from the favor of the crown a peerage and a poſt for life, of £.5000 a year for himſelf, and a ſplendid employ,

ploy, with an appointment of £.4000 per an-
num for his nephew and heir at law, &c. &c.
can publicly declare he has no place, penſion
or reverſion: and the one is I think a proper
ſupport to the other. They make upon any
occaſion a graceful alliance and very good
companions, as pictures of patriotiſm, to
hang or (if you like that better) to *lye* together, in the political way.

But, now *G——*, let me ſay a word to your
elaborate pamphlet upon the ſtamp act ; the
ſingle unfortunate eſſay of a late miniſter in
his late celebrated province of financierſhip.
And here, *in limine*, I ought not to conceal
from you what the world ſays——it comes
too late, it ſhould have accompanied the fu-
neral proceſſion wherein you make ſo admi-
rable a lugent figure : beſides it is too dear,
and too tedious. A man muſt, in truth,
like myſelf be ſadly put to it, before he can
go through a thick volume on ſuch a ſubject.
The author may perhaps have ſung to himſelf this ditty, *his ſaltem accumulem donis*, for-
getting the *fungar inani munere*. I declare I
could hardly keep open my eyes in reading
it, and the only thing that excited my ſur-
priſe was, how the devil two or three tole-
rably ſmart quotations ſhould have found
their way into the book. I know you had
no taſte for theſe *lumina dicendi* ; and as to
your *Newfoundland* ſpaniel, the little *German*
conſiderer, I think ſuch gaieties could never
iſſue from his ſqueaking pipe; and your other
ſecretary

fecretary is too pompous for levities like thefe, he is above being witty, never deviating farther than hiftorical parody at the moft. In fact, fome light-headed fellow, that by mere accident lit upon this large heavy piec : whilft it was kneading, muft have flung in thefe two or three grains of falt, at a time when the ferious maker was himfelf bufied about fome collateral matter, perhaps tying on the appendix.

Altho', I confefs, I got through the whole at laft, yet I fhall not put down all that occured to me in the perufal, having no right to tell *the public* as you do, that they *fhould hear*, *at leaft whilft I plead.* Indeed, I fhall content myfelf with taking things as they ftand upon your own reprefentation ; as it feems to me, notwithftanding the unfair and partial ftate of the evidence, that enough is difclofed by the writer to furnifh an anfwer to himfelf.

I fhall firft obferve, that the number of men we paid for the defence of America during the war, or the expence we were at, is no more to be placed to its fole account, than the charges we may fuftain in any war occafioned by a particular branch of trade is to be layed upon that. War is a general burthen, whatever may give rife to it. And we certainly thought the great trade carried on between England and its plantations in America, fo much for the benefit of the former that no expence was too great to fupport it. Indeed it was allowed to be of more worth to us than all the trade we have with the whole world befides.　　　　E　　　　In-

Indubitably it is a principle of government that " *Jupport* is due in return for protection" (that is) in liberty and property. But in the prefent inftance we really protected our own trade by protecting the colonies ; befides they *did* contribute largely to the maintenance of the war, and *do* fo to the expence of government. But, if it were reafonable that they fhould bear more of the burthen, it would have been but fair to apply to them for fuch contibution in the ufual aud accuftomed manner.

The quantum of the tax is not the object of confideration upon this head, " whether it be " half a day's labour or not ; nor whether the " advantages derived to the Americans from " two or three bounties given to them on " two or three articles, or the increafe of the " eftablifhment there, will enable them to " fupport the new impofitions." But whether the *Britifh* parliament or their own affemblies fhould lay the tax.

Nay, the foregoing pofitions, whether true or not, will not prove the propriety of the tax itfelf ; for, altho' the fum to be raifed were moderate, yet the manner of raifing it, and the particular things and people from whence it was to be raifed, might be injudicious, improper and inadequate.

Seeing our legiflature have declared our right to bind *America* by all forts of laws, I fhall not now queftion the foundations of that right ; but, the propriety of exercifing it, as

of

of late, is ftill open to confideration, and whether it fhould ever in prudence be recurred to
but in the laft refort.

Now, it was known that many prejudices
(if you will call them fo) were entertained
by the *Americans* againft this power, fo that
the miniftry could have no doubt but that
the attempt to put it in ufe would be odious
if not dangerous.

The *Americans*, as defcended from *Britons*
and communicating perpetually with them,
have always fancied they were entitled to the
fame privileges, and amongft the reft to that
of taxing themfelves; in fhort, from confidering themfelves as unreprefented in the *Britifh*
parliament, and that the rights of taxation
and reprefentation are infeparable, they have
regarded their own affemblies as eftablifhed
in its ftead, and therefore as one of the cor-
ner ftones of their conftitution.

Now this I do not much wonder at ; for,
excepting one great lawyer, I never heard any
man declare that the " principle of reprefentation neither is nor ever was a principle of
our government;" and this declaration too
carried the lefs weight with it for being accompanied with another, that " Mr. *Locke*,
in his treatife on government was the firft
perfon who ftarted the notion, which treatife
was a mere political pamphlet of the time
wherein the writer confidered what fhould be,
and not what was the conftitution of this
realm." Such doctrine moreover could not

be

be supposed sufficient to satisfy the *Americans*, seeing our statute book, and a multitude of writers evince the contrary. In fact, the notion of every man, who has any property, having a share in the legiflature of the country, by himself or by his representative, is undeniably evident in all the gothic conflitutions; and (to say nothing of the old *Britons* who had certainly their *conventus*;) it appears among our Saxons in their *witenagemot*, and *commune or generale concilium regni*, and also among the *Normans* who succeeded them. Indeed " legal and lasting property can never
" be ascertained in any community, unless
" each particular member, or at least each class
" of men, have either by themselves or proxy,
" some share in the legiflature; for, every man,
" in his deliberate proceedings, does naturally
" regard himself and only collaterally others,
" as their interest or concerns are interwoven
" with his own. Such then that are not
" immediately in person, or mediately by their
" representatives, some way concerned in the
" making laws will be most assuredly oppress-
" ed. When the *Saxons* first settled here, they
" regarded these two things, (1st.) that the
" whole community should be consulted in things
" of moment (2d.) that an order amongst them
" should be established upon tenure, for in
" this their safety, in regard to outward dan-
" ger confisted. *William* the Conqueror (who
" only made some small changes in the forms
" and in the posselfors of things) settled the
" force

" force intirely upon the land, by way of
" fervice, and thofe lands were in the hands
" of the Barons. The then fcarcity of money
" admitted of fmall or no impofitions, the
" rents being payed in provifion. For which
" reafon it is propable the great men only,
" who had the land, were for fome time
" after the conqueft confulted, as being the
" only perfons that contributed to the public
" by their fervices. But afterwards, as per-
" fonal wealth increafed, others being able
" to contribute, although they had little
" or no lands, were likewife confulted.
" And from thefe and fuch like reafons, it is
" propable the towns were firft fummoned to
" confult about the common affairs, and to
" give their affiftance to the common charge,
" and thereby eafe the land that was burden-
" ed with fervices. And perhaps from the
" fame reafon, the fole right of giving money
" came gradually into the hands of the com-
" mons ; for, the great men, being in pof-
" feffion of the tenures performed their per-
" fonal fervices which were annexed to their
" tenures, and fo it is probable in thofe early
" times contributed nothing in money (unlefs
" they compounded with the king for their
" fervices;) whereas the commoners, having but
" little land or no fervices, contributed money.
" And as the wealth and power of the com-
" monalty increafed, and fo the nature of
" the government gradually changing, they
" became the fole givers, (as they were the
" firft)

" firſt) of the money. For all *private perſons* hav-
" ing *a property* in this conſtitution (excepting
" ſuch as held in villanage of the great men,
" what was theirs was not to be diſpoſed of,
" without their conſent; for which reaſon
" whoever was taxed was ſomeway conſulted.
" And from the ſame reaſons, the repreſen-
" tatives of the towns, in proceſs of time, came
" to be ſo multiplied as to make four-fifths
" of the houſe of commons ; for, the barons,
" which were the greateſt proprietors in the
" land, were a diſtinct body. But under the
" reign of Henry the ſeventh, the circum-
" ſtances of the kingdom by trade and perſonal
" wealth being greatly changed, and the au-
" thority of the commons greatly increaſed,
" they were by virtue of his laws let into
" the land. And this affords us a hint how
" it came to paſs that in our government the
" number of repreſentatives of the great
" towns ſo far exceed thoſe of the land or
" counties in the Houſe of Commons. For
" the wealth being in thoſe early times for the
" moſt part perſonal, which was poſſeſſed by
" thoſe who traded and ſo lived in the great
" towns, and theſe being to contribute to the
" public charge, were therefore conſulted.
" Whereas, the greateſt part of the land, be-
" ing in the hands of the barons, who ap-
" peared in their own perſons in theſe aſſem-
" blies, and who were obliged by their
" tenures to ſervices, there then ſeemed not
to

" to have been required many reprefentatives
" for the land." But be thefe matters in
antient times as they will, it is clear that the
very preamble to the firft ftatute of James the
Ift. acknowledging his title (tho' penned
in a fulfome flattering ftrain) declares that
" there can be no means or ways fo fit for
" his faithful fubjects of all eftates and de-
" grees to agnize their loyalty as in the high
" court of parliament, where all the whole
" body of the realm, and *every particular*
" *member thereof, either by perfon or by repre-*
" *fentation (upon their own free elections)* are ·
" by the laws of this realm deemed to be
" perfonally prefent."

Lord Ch. J. *Coke* too (4 Inft. 1, 2) lays
down that " The Knights, Citizens and
" Burgeffes reprefent all the commons of the
whole realm and are trufted for them; and
" (p. 14.) when any new device is moved
" on the king's behalf in parliament, for his
" aid, or the like, the commons may anfwer
" that they dare not agree without conference
" with their countries."

Spelman (whofe book was publifhed in 1663,
tho' written long before) fpeaking of the manner of making laws, fays " Rex confilio &
" affenfu baronum fuorum leges *olim* impofuit
" univerfo regno, & contentire inferior
" quifq; vifus eft, in perfona Domini fui ca-
" pitalis, prout *hodie* per procuratores comi-
" tatus vel burgi, quos in parlamentis *knights*
" *& burgeffes* appellamus."

In

In the difcourfe on government, publifhed by *Bacon* foon after the death of *Charles* the 1ft. and fuppofed to be Mr. *Seiden's*, it is faid " the power of the commons in public councils was of fome efficacy, but not much honor, for their meetings were tumultuary ; time brought forth a cure thereof, the flowers of the people are by *election* fent to be the *reprefentative*.

And, I fuppofe, I need not mention *Hooker*, *Sidney*, *Neville*, and many other celebrated writers who held the fame language before the revolution.

Sidney indeed not only afferts this reprefentation, but argues for the neceffity of it to the raifing of money in a free government, fince " no man can give that which is anothers."

Commines, the *French* hiftorian, likewife takes notice, that it is the privilege of *Englifhmen* to pay nothing but with their own confents ; and *Fortefcue*, who lived in the reign of *Edward* the 4th, fays the fame thing in his treatife of government.

But a ftronger proof than the uniform doctrine of thefe writers, arifes from the feveral fucceffive acts of parliament relative to the principality of *Wales* and the palatinates of *Chefter* and *Durham*, &c. by which reprefentatives are exprefly given to thofe fubordinate ftates, becaufe " it is juft, equal and agreeable to the conftitution that they fhould have fuch, if they are to be liable to all payments, rates and

and fubfidies equally with the other inhabitants of the kingdom who have their knights
and burgeffes;" the 34 and 35 H. 8. running
in thefe words " that all the king's fubjects
" and refiants in *Wales*, fhall find at all parlia-
" ments *hereafter to be holden* in *England*,
" knights, citizens and burgeffes, according to
" the act in that cafe provided, and *fhall be
" charged and chargeable to all fubfidies and
" other charges to be granted* by the commons
" of any of the faid parliaments." Thefe therefore are fo many facts proving the general doctrine.

And here I do not believe you will complain of my not mentioning an anterior ftatute
taxing *Wales*, which was publicly cited by a
certain lawyer ; becaufe you know it could
not afterwards be found, nor indeed any traces
of it, either in the ftatute book or in the re-
cords of the *tower*, and therefore, altho' it
got fome how into that gentleman's notes, if
ever it had any other being, the fame has by
time diffolved,

And like the bafelefs fabric of a vifion
Left not a wreck behind.

But I am rather inclined to think it was
only a delufion, or creature of *fecond fight* ab-
origine, and therefore at beft but *argumentum*

F   *ad*

ad ignorantiam. For which reafon I am ex-
cufable for laying no ftrefs upon it.

The argument your writer adduces againft
this principle of the *Britifh* conftitution is, " if
" the legiflature has no power but over thofe
" who vote for the election of members, 1
" twentieths of the inhabitants of *Great-Bri-*
" *tain* are releaf.d from their fubjection ;"
and again " the commons of *Great-Britain*
" affembled in parliament, are not only the re-
" prefentatives of the counties and boroughs
" who depute them, but of all the commons
" of the realm." Now this is but very incon-
clufive reafoning ; for it is faying that, becaufe
we have not a compleat reprefentation, therefore we are intitied *of right* to none, but the
converfe of this propofition would be more
juft: and the truth is, that formerly all men who
had property of their own, and did not hold
at the will of the lord, and could pay towards
the public expence, were reprefented but by
the natural change in property, there are now
people who have feveral fpecies of it that are
not concerned in elections at all, nay many
large towns have fprung up which fend no
members, and feveral antient places are depo-
pulated which ftill continue to be reprefented.
Wherefore, reafoning upon the principle of
fublata caufa tollitur effectus, one might very
well fay fince property and the holders of it,
have in fome particulars changed their nature,

fo

fo it is high time, to change in fome particulars the regulations for their reprefentation,
in order to keep up to the true principles of
the conftitution. Nay, Mr. *Neville* in his
Plato Redivivus, publifhed in 1680, and lord
Molefworth in his preface to *Franco Gallia*,
as well as other writers, have long ago
touched upon this point, and infifted that
" towns becoming defolate, as *old Sarum*,
" will deferve to lofe the right of fending re-
" prefentatives to parliament, and to have
" their deputies transferred to better peopled
" places, worthy (through their numbers
" and wealth) of being reprefented. For
" certainly a wafte or defart has no right
" to be reprefented, nor by our original con-
" ftitution was ever intended to be."

Now the *Americans* do not fay that they
are imperfectly reprefented, but that they
are not reprefented at all, in *England*; infomuch that no freeholder or member of any
corporation in all *America* has by virtue thereof any capacity for fitting or voting for any
reprefentative in parliament; and that therefore it is they have hitherto, from their very
firft eftablifhment, for more than 100 years,
uniformly exercifed and enjoyed the privilege
of impofing and raifing their own taxes,
in their provincial affemblies, of which they
choofe the members. So that they look

upon

upon themfelves now to be not only intitled
thereto by the principles of the *Britifh* government, but by an uninterrupted ufage fufficient of itfelf to make a conftitution. For
the prefent inhabitants contend that they have
inherited this franchife of raifing money upon
themfelves from their anceftors. And then
they afk, what they have done to forfeit thefe
their antient liberties and immunities, and
when it is that they have refufed to grant any
aids that have been properly applied for ? Nay,
your own writer fays, that " *Penfylvania* vot-
" ed in Sep. 1765, *Nem. Con.* That whenever
" his majefty fhall require the aids of the in-
" habitants of the province, and they fhall
" be called upon for that purpofe in a confti-
" tutional way, it will be *their indifpenfible*
" *duty* to grant their proportion for the *Britifh*
" *American* provinces."

Suppofing therefore the right of *England,*
and fuppofing alfo that it was requifite to
levy a revenue upon *America* for the ufe of
the ftate in general ; Why was it neceffary,
feeing it was certainly imprudent and odious,
to levy it now, for the firft time, in an unufual
manner by force of an *Englifh* ftatute, without laying the matter before the feveral *A-
merican* affemblies, and feeing whether they
would not raife it themfelves ? For, after
people

people have long enjoyed any prerogative, especially that of granting their own money and giving a part of their estates, or (as we more emphatically express it) of making *free gifts*, it is scarcely possible to withdraw it without murmur, nay without tearing it from them by force, and at the expence of a civil war, if they have the means of supporting one. Therefore, causelessly, one would imagine, no wise administration would attempt it.

This I do not say from history alone, or from what has lately happened, (nor do I gather it from the excellent pamphlet published in *America* upon the occasion by Mr. *Delany*, nor from any recent writings or proceedings) but from particular grounds that our ministers must have been acquainted with before the stamp act could be thought of. For, in 1754, when the war was breaking out in *America*, a plan was formed there for its defence and for defraying the unavoidable expences to that end, which was transmitted hither, but, not being approved, a new one was sent from hence, whereby the governors were to be impowered to draw for money upon the treasury here, and the treasury to be reimbursed by a tax laid on the colonies by act of parliament. This when it arrived, was communicated by governor *Shirley* to a

man

man of great confideration at *Philadelphia*, whofe remarks at that time had fo much weight with the then miniftry, as to occafion its being laid afide, and this too was *before* the *French* power in that country was fubdued. The remarker faid, he apprehended the taxing *Americans* by act of parliament, would give extreme diffatisfaction, and urged the following reafons againft it. " In matters of general con- " cern to the people, and efpecially where bur- " thens are to be laid upon them, it is of ufe " to confider as well what they will be apt to " think and fay, as what they ought to think. " They will fay that the parliament of *Great* " *Britain* is at a great diftance, · fubject to be " mifinformed and mifled ; that it is fuppofed " an undoubted right of *Englifhmen* not to be " taxed but by their own confent, given " through their reprefentatives ; that the " colonies have no reprefentatives in parlia- " ment ; that compelling the colonies to " pay money without their confent would be " rather like raifing contributions in an " enemy's country, than taxing *Englifhmen* " for their own public benefit ; that it would " be treating them as a conquered people, and " not as true *Britifh* fubjects, and that if it be " done, their affemblies may be difmiffed as an " ufelefs part of the conftitution." At the fame time he fpeaks of thofe fecondary taxes which

which are layed on exports, and imports, and of
the reftraints on manufacturing. as what has
been cuftomary, and therefore chearfully fubmitted to. As indeed the power of doing this
feems to be a neceffary attendant on the fovereignty of government, which by keeping
the keys, the fhips and fortreffes of the ftate,
muft have the confequent power of letting in
or letting out what commodities they pleafe,
and upon what terms; and which general
fuperintendency of the whole empire muft alfo
entitle it to prefcribe how and in what manner
and to what degree the productions of any
part fhall be manufactured. But the taking
from them their poffeffions, or the produce
thereof (not merely forbidding certain ufes of
it,) nay the very money out of their pockets
without their own confent, is what they would
confider as oppreffion and inconfiftent with
being freemen.

I wifh therefore with all my heart we had
been contented with impofing thefe fecondary
taxes, and had left the raifing of money to
their own affemblies; being fully aware how
improvident and infatuated a minifter muft be
that would force on a meafure of government
unneceffarily, which muft unavoidably lead
to the difcuffion of points that fhould never
be

be brought into queſtion, and which if once diſputed muſt be attended with dangerous conſequences at the leaſt.

Beſides, if a like thing had never been done whilſt the Colonies were young ; was it prudent to ſet about it now, that they were numerous in people, accuſtomed to arms and extended in territory, after having recently diſbanded ſeveral regiments among them, and diſpoſed of lands to the officers and ſoldiers that compoſed them ? Strange and unhappy politics ſurely !

But let our force have been ever ſo predominant and irreſiſtible ; as the *Engliſh* parliament had never interfered before in levying a revenue from *America*, there was in appearance ſomething cruel and overbearing in touching their purſes now, without communicating with them about the occaſion. And if, as your writer more than once inſinuates, the product of the ſtamp-act, was really to be applied to *American* purpoſes, it ſeems to have been the ſtrangeſt policy in the world not to have conſulted them, becauſe nobody can doubt but they would have contributed to every reaſonable requeſt for their own benefit. The moſt gracious way of doing things is the beſt, as nothing can excuſe

harſh

harſh meaſures but neceſſity. One muſt therefore conclude from this writer that our ill-fated
miniſter chuſing " to hold the rein with a
firm hand," treated our colonies in an arbitrary manner, when it anſwered no end to do
ſo, merely becauſe it was his favourite method
of driving on government. And this will account likewiſe for the antipathy he every
where expreſſes to lawyers.

Indeed, if this revenue were ultimately de-
ſigned for *American* uſes, who could be ſo
proper judges of thoſe as themſelves ?

Moreover, no perſons know ſo well as the
people furniſhing the money, in what way
they can raiſe it with moſt eaſe, which is likewiſe a conſideration of ſome weight with a
wiſe treaſury.

And above all, it ſeems to have been imprudent, when we were exerting, for the firſt
time, our right of laying an internal tax upon
America, to accompany it with the deprivation
of another privileg - that is generally much valu-
ed, that of the trial by jury. It was, to recur to

G   your

your own figure, uſing the *rein* too freely at the outſet.

Having ſaid thus much with reſpect to the manner of doing the thing, I will make ſome few obſervations on the matter itſelf.

The act directs that the tax ſhall be paid in ſterling money of *Great Britain,* and remitted to the Exchequer in *England.* Now, in ſome provinces, it is very well known, there is no money at all, but paper money ; therefore in that reſpect there was a natural impoſſibility of executing the act. In other provinces ſpecie was very rare, and by the new orders ſent out by the ſame miniſtry prohibiting the importation of *Spaniſh* Bullion, (almoſt the only ſpecie that comes there) this ſcarcity was every day increaſing. This laſt, therefore, was a regulation of trade tending directly to defeat the act ; for, the requiring the tax to be paid in ſpecie, and the prohibiting the only ſpecie current, was literally the requiring of bricks to be made without ſtraw : It was of a piece with the politics of *Laputa,* where after diligent ſtudy on the means of improving the old methods of tillage, they turned pigs into their fields to ſave the article of plough-

ploughing, although every body elfe knew
that where thofe animals have once rooted the
ground with their nofes, nothing will afterwards grow, and the confequence accordingly
was an unufual dearth of the very thing the
minifters wanted moft to produce.

Befides, if, as the pamphleteer advances, the money to be raifed was to be layed out in *America,*
no reafon can be affigned why the act fhould
command it to be tranfmitted to the Treafury here ; unlefs it were to give the miniftry an
opportunity of difplaying their tory principles in
difpenfing with the pofitive words of a ftatute
by a Treafury order. This, however was, it
feems, intended ; for your apologift fays, " It
" would have calmed the fears that the colo-
" nies would be drained of their fpecie,
" if the directions had been iffued which
" the Treafury, *July* 9, 1765, (by their mi-
" nute) had given, That the produce of the
" *American* duties arifing by virtue of any
" *Britifh* act of parliament, fhould be paid to
" the deputy paymafter in *America* to defray
" the fubfiftence of the troops and any milita-
" ry expences incurred in the colonies."

G 2   And

And yet the ſtatute poſitively enacts, " That all the monies ſhall be paid into the " receipt of his Majeſty's Exchequer, and ſhall " be entered ſeparate and apart from all other " monies, and ſhall be there reſerved to be " from time to time diſpoſed of by the par- " liament.

And " That if the commiſſioners for ma-- " naging the ſaid duties, or the receiver ge-- " neral ſhall neglect or refuſe to pay into the " Exchequer all or any of the ſaid monies, " or ſhall divert, or miſapply any part there- " of ; then they, and every of them ſo of-- " fending, ſhall be liable to pay double the " value." Now, I cannot (I ſuppoſe) ſpeak to the ſtamp-author in any language more un-exceptionable than his own, and therefore I ſhall ſay " The power of judging whether or " no an act of parliament ſhall be carried " into execution, is not by the conſtitution in- " truſted to any miniſtry. The bill of rights " declares the pretended power of ſuſpending " of laws, or the execution of laws, by regal " authority, without conſent of parliament, " is illegal." Indeed one main topic for his abuſe of the ſucceeding miniſtry, is their deli-berating in council (in purſuance of the King's orders)

orders) upon the intelligence received from *America* of an oppofition to the ftamp act, and on what was moft fit to be done in confequence thereof. Where, after telling us that " the privy council report hereupon, that this " is a matter of the utmoft importance to the " trade and legiflature of *Great Britain,* and " of too high a nature for the determination " of your majefty in your privy council, and " is proper only for the confideration of par- " liament," he fays, " The execution of the " laws is refted in the king, and dele- " gated by him to the officers in each depart- " ment, the privy council cannot deliberate " upon the laws, tho' they can affift the exe- " cution of them; and the principle which at- " tributes to the king in council the power " of difpenfing with the laws of the land, is " the higheft treafon againft the ftate." Now if this be fo, I humbly conceive a board of treafury has not a fuperior power, and then I leave the confequence to be drawn by himfelf.

With refpect to the tax itfelf. A ftamp on all private fecurities, on all proceedings in courts of law for the recovery of juft debts, and on all the neceffary tranfactions in merchandize

chandize and fhipping, &c. is a great burthen
and clog to any country, and exceedingly oppreffive and injurious to an infant ftate. It is
one of the laft taxes that was thought of a-
mong us, and has been only by degrees in the
courfe of the laft 70 years extended to the feveral articles now loaded with it. But the late
financier, fo far from confidering this, has at
once impofed a ftamp in *America* upon every
thing that pays it in this country; nay, has
carried it farther by laying it there upon clearances of fhips outwards.

To crown the whole, the profecutions and
informations for the non-payment of this
tax, were to be had in courts exceedingly diftant, where no jury is ufed, where the judges
are intitled to fees and poundage on convic-
tion, and hold their offices during pleafure;
the appeal for any grievance is to be made to
a court of this fort; and none lies to the quarter
feffions as in *England:* fo that no redrefs is
to be expected; or, if to be obtained, can be
worth the expence of procuring.

But

But this difeafe in the act is likewife to be
cured by our author's conftant *noftrum*, a
treafury prefcription ; for, he fays " There
" was a memorial from the Treafury dated
" *July* the 4th, 1765, prefented to his majefty
" in council, ftating the expediency of giving
" the judges in *America* fufficient and honoura_
" ble falaries in lieu of fees and all poundage,
" and of eftablifhing *three* different courts
" of vice-admiralty, with proper diftricts to
" each." A very adequate remedy truly !
But, one cannot help remarking that even
this and the other miferable palliative, were
never thought of till the expiration of the
miniftry's power ; for, this is dated the 4th,
and the former the 9th of *July*, and the pamphleteer fays that " the intention to change
" the miniftry was declared in *May*, and
" their fucceffors came into office in the
" beginning of *July*." So that thefe treafury
legacies of an oppreffive minifter, like the
death-bed charities of an ufurer, were to be
carried into execution by thofe that came after, and feem rather the effect of dying fears,

or

or an artifice for leaving a good name behind, than the product of any good principle.

This now is an unaggravated reprefenta- tion of this unexampled act, which I confefs feems to me calculated to alarm every man who had but heard of a *Britifh* conftitution, and much more who thought he was intitled to the benefits of it.

Your writer cannot vary the ftate of the cafe. But he fays that the financier who projected this act, " after the refolutions " come to in 1764, gave a year's delay, that " any information might be received from " *America*, with regard to the *Expediency* " of the tax propofed, not to permit the right " of impofing it to be controverted." He then gives us room to conclude, that before the end of this year, the *Americans* had in their affemblies difputed our right of taxing them, and fays in a note that " on the 11th of " *December*, 1764, the board of trade " reported to the king that the affemblies

of

" of Maffachufet's Bay and New York, had
" treated the acts and refolutions of the legi-
" flature with the moft indecent difrefpect."
And here he fupprefles, what he knows
likewife to be a fact, that fome of our governors there, and particularly Mr. Bernard, reprefented ftrongly againft the projected meafure, and that feveral other remonftrances
againft it couched in the moft inoffenfive
manner, came from many parts of America,
and that this Report and *all thefe papers*
were laid before the Privy Council. He
goes on, " The Privy Council advifed the
" King to give directions that the fame
" be layed before parliament, at *fuch time*
" *and in fuch manner as his majefty fhould be*
" *pleafed to direct and appoint."* And then
adds, not very logically, " *This poftponed* the
" laying *it* before parliament, *as it was meant*
" *to do* ; but it deprived parliament of no in-
" formation; for the affemblies had inftructed their agents here to prepare petitions
" *in the fame words*, and particularly Mr.
" Mauduit the agent for Maffachufet's Bay
" was directed to draw his principles and
" argument from Mr. Otis's book. Pe-
" titions were prefented, afferting the right
" of freedom from taxes impofed by Great
" Britain. Thefe were rejected by par-
" liament, not from ignorance of their
" contents but becaufe their contents
" were known; becaufe they denied the
" power of G. B. No information *there-*
" *fore* was witheld by this delay, the caufe
" of which was tendernefs to the Colonies.
H   " For

" For, had the king called the attention
" of parliament to proceedings in which
" their acts were treated with the moft in-
" decent difrefpect, their own dignity muft
" have drawn from them votes of cenfure
" and feverity towards the offenders: and
" therefore the miniftry, who were taking
" the proper methods to form and enforce
" the act, witheld *a paper*, which would
" have given no information but what was
" given in a manner lefs calculated to irri-
" tate mens minds."

Such a fpecimen of reafoning (I believe)
can hardly be produced fince the ufe of the
pen has been known. And who would
think a man fit to be at the head of an adminiftration, who could put together fuch
inconfequential matter, after beginning his
pamphlet in this manner. " It is time that
" the public fhould receive the evidence
" which has hitherto been induftrioufly con-
" cealed from them; having heard the claims
" of America, they fhould hear, *at leaft*
" *whilft I plead*, the caufe of Great Britain."
For, from this exordium any man living
would conclude that the American claims
(or petitions as he afterwards calls them)
had been largely heard, even by council
at the bar of parliament, and that people
in general had been fo ftrongly impreffed
thereby that none could be heard who were
inclined to gainfay them ; whilft we Englifhmen had not a foul to urge a fyllable
on our fide of the queftion, and that by
                                        fome

some means or other all the evidence too
that made for us was induſtriouſly concealed.
And yet this laſt muſt rather ſeem unaccountable to the reader who knew that the
miniſter (an hearty Engliſhman) with a
great majority was ſtrongly bent upon carrying the meaſure into execution. Why,
in fact, the aſſertion is falſe, the very reverſe
was notoriouſly the caſe ; and, what is ſtill
more unaccountable than the aſſertion itſelf,
this very writer in his ſubſequent narrative
(as the reader muſt have remarked in the
paſſages cited above) tells you ſo himſelf,
and pretends alſo to give the true reaſon
for it.

But here I muſt beg leave particularly
to draw your attention to the note which
ſays, the Privy Council gave directions to lay
what was received from America before parliament *at ſuch time as his Majeſty ſhould
appoint,* and that *this poſtponed the laying it
before them, as it was meant to do.*

For, to avoid, I ſuppoſe, either telling
fairly the truth, or affirming unequivocally
what the writer knew to be falſe, he has
here conveyed himſelf in ſuch dark and im-
perfect expreſſions, that the reader muſt ſup-
ply ſeveral words to compleat the ſenſe.
And having done this, the aſſertion will then
be — " The miniſtry originally intended to
lay every thing before parliament, but the
Privy Council ordering them to take his
Majeſty's directions as to the time of doing
ſo and the waiting for theſe directions from
his

his Majesty, who either from indifference or disinclination delayed giving any, postponed the matter indefinitely, and thereby prevented the intentions of the ministry from taking effect." This must be the real sense; but then the writer knew it to be untrue, and that the real fact was a very criminal one, no less than a willful suppression by the ministry themselves of important evidence which the Privy Council had directed them particularly to lay before parliament; and therefore he has had recourse to indeterminate expressions in order to blunt its effect. The weak writer, however, had better have wholly omitted the mention of this transaction, instead of sliding it into a note only as it were by the bye, and giving himself so much torture about the expression of it. But, like guilt in a culprit, it hung somehow about his mind, and to ease that, he could not help betraying himself, altho' he had not honesty enough to make an ingenuous confession. His subterfuges and little artifices are really curious. In *the first place*, in order to represent the matter of little moment he puts it into a note, and denominates all that was comprised in the order of council *it*, (and afterwards *a paper)* although consisting of several different papers, such as votes, resolutions, letters of advice and intelligence from governors and officers, remonstrances, &c. with the report of the board of trade thereon. In the *next place* he endeavours to represent his Majesty
and

and the Privy Council, or at leaft his Majefty
(might he be permitted to fpeak the truth,)
as the real caufe of no information being layed
before the houfes, primarily perhaps the
Privy Council by giving directions that his
Majefty's pleafure fhould be taken as to the
time and manner of doing the fame, and
fecondarily his Majefty by never fignifying
his pleafure in that refpect at all; leaving
room to the reader to conjecture that it
might be the intention of the Minifters as
well as of the Privy Council to do it, but
that both were prevented by the King's
delaying to appoint any time for its being
done. Whereas the board of trade made
their report on the 11th of December, 1764,
and the Privy Council gave their advice
upon the matter foon afterwards, long before
the ftamp act came into the houfe. The
authority too of fo weighty a board as the
Privy Council always enforces and expedites,
inftead of retarding, any meafure. And it
is moreover fully known that his prefent
Majefty never puts off or defers any public
bufinefs. Had not the pamphleteer therefore
borne teftimony againft himfelf (as he does
in his pamphlet) I would venture to leave it
to any man's judgment whether a king, fo
fond of parliaments as our prefent fovereign,
would of himfelf be likely to delay for an
inftant the communicating there, any national matter, efpecially after his privy council
had advifed him fo to do; or whether a
miniftry who have been fo notorious for
fupporting

supporting themselves on points of law against courts of juftice were not very likely to difregard fuch advice and to exhort his Majefty not to follow it as it made againft their own meafure. The matter will not admit of a doubt. And therefore this writer is guilty of grofs difrefpect and obloquy as well as of untruth, in giving us to underftand that either the Council by directing the King's pleafure to be taken as to the time, or the King by not fignifying his pleafure, poftponed the laying thefe matters before parliament *as it was meant to do.* Which concluding words, I fhall in *the laft place* obferve, avoid faying directly by whom this was meant; although none but the miniftry could be the perfons here intended by the author. Now, this is the pooreft fhift of all. For, if the Privy Council direct willing minifters to do a thing, taking only his Majefty's pleafure as to the time and manner, and his Majefty (as we well know) be ever ready to enter upon bufinefs and to do his part in all acts of ftate; what fhould hinder the things being forthwith done? why then at laft, like a true confcious culprit, the writer after all this tergiverfation is obliged to difclofe the real fact, to wit, that " the miniftry, who were taking " the proper methods to form and enforce " the act witheld a paper," that is, all papers and all light whatever, from the parliament, who fhould have been poffeffed of the whole as *they* were to decide for

the

the public upon the matter. So that this paltry apologift muft finally be driven to explain away the words *as it was meant to do* either of other perfons than the miniftry or of fome other time, or elfe admit them to contain a downright falfity. Now, nobody elfe could be in the fituation of doing the thing in queftion, but the miniftry, and therefore it muft refer to them. Well then if they are the perfons, they muft have meant to do it *before* the report of the board of trade and the advice of the Privy Council and the taking of his Majefty's pleafure thereon, otherwife, thefe proceedings could not be faid to *poftpone it*; and if fo, he fhould have told us why the council were confulted at all upon the matter, feeing the minifters were refolved, from the beginning, not to hearken to their advice, unlefs it fell in with their own ways of thinking, and fhould alfo have mentioned this their intention as previous to, and put it *before* thofe proceedings and not in his narration have placed it *after*, as if fome fubfequent event had occafioned it. But he knows it was never their meaning and intention neither before, during, nor after the deliberation in council; and it was for that reafon he has chofen not to affert it of any particular men or time, but to affirm generally *it was meant*, in fuch neutral words as may lead an ofcitant reader into a doubt, whether there was not fuch a meaning at fome time or other, even after the advice of the Privy Council upon

the

the fubject : and indeed if a man is com-
pelled to lie in his defence, he is prudent
in ufing the moſt equivocal terms he can,
becaufe then an unwary reader may be impofed upon, and as to a wary one, although
the lie be couched fhortly and lurk in few
words, yet to detect the falfehood and lay
it fairly open, he will be obliged perhaps
to be long and will therefore rather give up
the tafk than be at the pains that are requifite for the purpofe.

Having however been at this trouble, and
pretty well probed this notable paffage, I
fhall now confider a little more fully the
fact it relates to, and which has occafioned
all this duplicity.

The financier of the kingdom projects an
internal tax upon its colonies, the firft that
ever was laid, and, by way of feeling the
pulfe of mankind upon it, comes to a refolution for the purpofe a year before it is
to be actually laid, that is, in the fpring of
1764. All the colonies are thereupon alarmed and come to votes denying our right to
lay fuch a tax ; fome of our ableft governors there, particularly Mr. Bernard, reprefent againſt the advifablenefs of fuch a
meafure, feveral remonftrances are made
againſt it, and many letters upon the fubject,
come from America. They are laid before
the board of trade, which reports thereon
in December 1764. The matter being of
infinite moment to the nation in general ;
the whole is referred by the King to his
council,

council, and the council advise his Majefty to lay the fame before the parliament: the miniftry diffuade his Majefty from complying with this advice and prevail. This is the naked fact, and it is not only of the firft impreflion, but of fo daring a nature, that it is not to be paralleled in hiftory. The infatuation of the financier is perfectly amazing. He, as the minifter projecting the tax, being a member of the Privy Council, urges there whatever he can againft the communication of any lights from America to Parliament, but, notwithftanding the weight of all his arguments and his influence, as minifter, thrown into the fcale, the board deem the matter of fo much confequence to the nation that they pofitively order him to acquaint the King that they recommend it to his Majefty to lay the fame before parliament. The hardy projector not being able to prevent fuch advice from going to the throne, prefumes, even there, to obtrude his own opinion againft that of the council board. Now, no reafon can be given for this proceeding of his, but a perfuafion that the parliament would, had thefe lights been given to them, have rejected his fcheme. And that being fo, let me afk whether any thing more wrong-headed, nay more violent and wicked, could be practifed? For, what can be a more enormous offence in a minifter againft his country, than a wilfull fecretion of evidence from its legiflature, in a matter whereon they are to decide

I   what

what is of the utmoft moment to the whole
ftate ; and more efpecially after the Privy
Council had examined and found it to be fo
important as to direct exprefsly its being laid
before them ?

If fuch a proceeding as this is not a matter of impeachment, I know not what is,
and therefore nothing furprizes me fo much
as the infatuation of minifters who could
confefs fo much guilt, unlefs it be the fu-
pinenefs of thofe who could hear fuch a
confeffion and not immediately move an impeachment upon it—the crime atrocious and
the criminals hardily avowing it. The fact
will (I fear) fcarcely be believed hereafter
when hiftory relates it ; for, there are very
few feafons when fo daring a breach of the
conftitution, and fo grofs a betraying of a
minifter's duty to the public and to the
whole legiflature of his country, could have
paffed with impunity and efcaped the ven-
geance that is due to it. The magnitude of
the offence, I fuppofe, became its protection;
the fucceeding miniftry not adding intire
faith even to what was confeffed, fo incredi-
ble is enormous flagitioufnefs to men of virtue and real patriotifm.

But to refume my fubject. The ftamp
author not only confutes his exordium in
what I have already cited (for I take every
thing from himfelf) but he repeats the fame
matter afterwards by faying " in the begin-
" ning of 1765, feveral petitions, which
" denied the right of impofing taxes on the
" colonies

" colonies were prefented and were *therefore*
" rejected." The reafon however which he
here alledges as well as before, why they
were rejected, is not the true one, as I have
been informed. Nay, it could not be fo;
For, fome of the petitions were worded very
guardedly, avoided faying a fyllable againft
our right, and confined themfelves to the
propriety, expediency and feafibility of the
tax. Thefe therefore could not be rejected
for the reafon fuggefted; neither is it true
that " the affemblies had inftructed their
" agents here to *prepare petitions in the fame*
" *words.*" For, the very inftance, which this
inconfiftent writer brings in proof of it,
proves the contrary, namely, " that Mr.
" *Mauduit* was directed to draw his princi-
" ples and arguments from Mr. *Otis's* book;"
becaufe if Mr. *Mauduit* prepared a petition
in the fame words, with that which his
conftituents had offered, he muft copy theirs
verbatim, and then he could not do what
they directed, draw one himfelf from another fource, that is, from Mr. *Otis's*
large (and let me add) very ill-written and
confufed treatife.

What Mr. *Mauduit* did in confequence of
this direction it is not material to enquire;
but, be what it would it was fo little agreeable to the province for which he was agent,
that they difmiffed him from their fervice
foon after.

The report of the day was, as I recollect,
that the unperfuadable minifter at that un-
fortun.

fortunate period infifted upon the American ftamp bill being a money bill, therefore no petition againft it could by the rules
of parliament be received, and that upon
this ground all the petitions from the whole
continent of America and from the agents
of the feveral provinces were rejected, infomuch that not one of them all was either
read, heard, or layed in any way whatever
before parliament, the only court where
the *caufe* of America (to adopt your language) could be tried. It was confequently determined without being *pleaded* at all.
This however I am inclined to think was
no more than an oftenfible reafon, and
that the true one was the fame which the
ftamp author relied upon againft the Privy
Council, that is, *the miniftry were taking the
proper methods to form and enforce the act,*
which it is ten to one had either the Americans or their agents been heard, or had
the Privy Council been obeyed, would never have paffed; and then we fhould have
had no proof at all of our great financier's
abilities in his favorite department, which
would certainly have been a great mortifica-
tion and lofs to himfelf, whatever it might
have been to the public. But as it has
turned out, this fingle enterprize will af-
ford us a notable fample both of his capacity for finding out good funds and of his
firmnefs in adhering to them againft all oppofition, and has therefore (I believe) pretty
nearly united all mankind in one and the

fame

fame opinion concerning him. However, although I cannot help doing him the juftice to fay, that I look upon him to be quite original, in having fo manfully withftood the opinion of the Council board; yet I cannot allow him to be wholly fo, in fhutting out all the light, before he proceeded to a difcuffion of the matter; becaufe, if I miftake not, there was a certain French judge, celebrated by Rabelais, who faid, much in the fame ftyle, *Let us begin, if you pleafe, with laying the evidence out of the cafe.*

For my own part, I beg leave now, to revert to our writer to the ftamp act, for he merits further attention in the progrefs of his reafoning, and particularly, with refpect to the conclufion that he draws from the fecretion of the American proceedings, which had been before the Council. His firft pofition is, that " it deprived parliament of no " information," which he makes out by faying, " becaufe the agents of the Colonies " were inftructed to petition in the fame " words." And then he acquaints us, that thefe petitions of the agents were refufed to be admitted by the houfes. Wherefore his conclufion, that by the management of the miniftry the parliament was deprived of no information, is in my humble opinion fully proved.

To fpeak ferioufly, the bare ftate of what he fays, is fo pregnant with palpable abfurdity, that one does not know which to blame moft, his head or his heart. For no man before, I dare fay, ever maintained, that the exclufion of all evidence was no deprival of information.

However he more than once roundly afferts that although the parliament heard no reprefentation, or Council at all; yet, they knew as much of the matter as if they had ; the witholding of the American remonftrances and arguments, being the fame thing with him, as the communication of them; and then he fays, with equal good fenfe and truth, that the reafon of the whole not being laid before parliament, was, tendernefs to the Colonies : fo that there was much tendernefs fhewn to the Americans, by the miniftry, in not revealing that of them to the Parliament, which, according to him, it knew already, and in debarring them, by this means, from all opportunity of explaining, qualifying or defending what was moft exceptionable or offenfive in their feveral claims and petitions.

Is it poffible to couch   nd felf-contradiction upon paper   who is capable of lofing his time in arguing with fuch a legiflator would deferve no better fate than that of living under his government.

The writer takes for granted every where, that the Englifh parliament have a right to tax America, when and how they pleafe. Be it fo : yet furely there is fomething tyrannical in condemning men unheard.

The

The laying hold of any little parliamentary regulation of order, to exclude the reprefentation of fome millions of fubjects upon a matter that folely concerns them, feems at leaft to be hard. For no man as poffeffed of Britifh property will pay any part of what is impofed upon America; fo that the Britifh parliament by fubjecting the Americans to pay in taxes the whole of their worth would not fubject themfelves to the payment of one fingle farthing. Therefore no man in his fenfes can put the continent of America, populous, extenfive and diftant as it is, upon a footing with any individual or fingle corporation in England; feeing there is no fort of property in this ifland which any inhabitant can be poffeffed of, but that fome member of parliament has the like. Befides, nothing can pafs here in either houfe, but what immediate notice may be given of it to any part of the kingdom. Whereas all the property in the whole continent of America would not qualify any man to fit in the Englifh parliament, nor even to give a vote for any member of it : nor is it poffible during the progrefs of any bill in either houfe, or during any feffion, to have any communication with any part of that continent upon any matter whatever. In fact, no American has any thing more to do with the choice of our lower houfe of parliament, who are ftiled *the Reprefentatives* of the Commons of England, than with the Senate of Sweden.

The

The only means they have of laying any matter before either house, is by their agents, and when these are repulsed, for any informality or other reason, the provinces, who must be the sufferers, have no way of being heard and are remediless.

At least, no man of any bowels or prudence, in so grave and momentous a matter, as that of satisfying our Colonists we behave with all the indulgence towards them that the forms of our constitution will admit would, like the stamp-author, call them " the wanton Americans forming a con- " certed plan of obstinate rebellion"; be- cause they earnestly insist upon what they think their legal rights, and have, hitherto, been actually permitted to enjoy; and by this strain of writing, endeavour to raise an animosity here against them, by contrasting them with a fanciful picture of " the poor " English peasant, driven into a temporary " insurrection by the whip of that severest " master want, and taught to expect con- " dign punishment and speedy justice, from " the rigour and vigilance of government :" although our present considerate and bold ministers have just ventured to lay an em- bargo, in spight of a statute to the contra- ry, for their relief, and have thereby ex- posed themselves to much calumny from the same quarter. I am sure none of this conduct bespeaks a wise politician, who is desirous of establishing a character with the men of sense and observation in this country.

try. It is a fort of flippant oratory more
fuited to the fmall petulant genius of a
Cambridgefhire poet, who is ufed only as a
fiddle to a party, than to a man who aims at
being confidered as a proper head for ad-
miniftring the affairs of a great kingdom,
upon any change that may happen. Fun,
witticifm and humour are out of place, when
two thirds of the trade of the firft com-
mercial country in the world are thought, by
by many people, to be at ftake. And nothing lowers a confpicuous man, more than
his miftaking the proper objects of merri-
ment. In truth he muft be a contemptible
creature, who can make fport with the fuf-
ferings of mankind; and will, when he at-
tempts it, find that nobody will give him
credit any longer, for really feeling for his
own country, let him proteft it afterwards
as violently as he pleafes.

And I might fay the fame of caricatura,
or extravagant exaggeration, fuch as calling
America's claim to the fole right of taxing
herfelf, " a refufal to be fubject *at all* to
Great Britain," although fhe declares the
contrary, willingly fubmits to all her exter-
nal taxes and to her regulations in trade and
manufactures.

For a moment, let me now fuppofe the
fact to have been, that the Americans, by
moft of their petitions, infifted upon the
exclufive right of taxing themfelves. Might
not the Parliament have at once declared
their own right to tax America, and have
K   precluded

precluded council from arguing that point, but have let them into the difcuffion of the expediency of the tax itfelf? and might not fuch difcuffion have thrown fome lights upon the houfe, which it was deprived of? would it not at leaft have been indulgent, reconciling and truly paternal conduct?

The felf-fufficiency of the financier, made him, I know, defirous of rejecting all information, and yet fo convicted has he been fince, of the groffeft ignorance of the ftate of many of the American provinces, that it were to be wifhed he had not by his obftinacy proceeded as he did, and lighted a flame, which perhaps our pofterity may feel the effects of. It may well be deemed an ill ftarred act, if no other ill confequence flowed from this unfortunate fcheme for revenue, than the having alarmed all America, fo much and fo generally, that it produced, what was not possible, an union of the feveral jarring and difcordant governments or ftates, fo that they formed, for the firft time, a general congrefs. In fhort they confidered the matter as *commune periculum.* Every province took the alarm, and they all coalefced as one man againft a common enemy. What projects may take rife hereafter from this tafte of an *Amphyctionian* affembly, I will not prophefy; but the mifchief alone that may fpring from fuch a fource, will probably be more than all the fervices ten thoufand fuch minifters, as the author

thought

thor of the ſtamp act, will ever be able to do to his country. One ſuch proof, of a head ill turned for the adminiſtration of the concerns of this nation, is enough to extinguiſh any man for ever as a politician it muſt, and ought to act like a milliſtone round his neck.

But is it not wonderful that after all the evidence to the contrary, which the writer exhibits himſelf, he ſhould ſay, that " it " was the opinion of almoſt every officer " in America, that the act would be " obeyed."

The votes 11 Dec. 1764, of *Maſſachuſets Bay* and *New York*, would make any body apprehend the contrary. Nay, the act paſſed but the 22d, of March, 1765, and the pamphlet confeſſes p. 39 " the fulleſt ac- " counts were ſoon received of the tur- " bulent and ſeditious behaviour of a part " of America." Upon the 29th of May following, that is, within ſix weeks, Virginia came to reſolutions, " denying the " right of the parliament of Gr. B. to tax " that colony." Theſe very reſolutions arrived here the 27th of July (but a very little after the financier was, luckily for this kingdom and himſelf, diſcarded from his Majeſty's ſervice). " The Governor diſſolved " the aſſembly (p. 41) and from the intelli- " gence the miniſtry received of the ſtate of " the province, they ſaw that theſe reſolu- " tions were meant, not to be mere verbal " aſſertions

" affertions but *principles of action, &c.* and
" (p. 43—4.) that governmet was fet at open
" defiance." p. 50 mentions a letter dated
the enfuing Auguft whcrein the writer fays,
" two or three months ago I thought
" that people would have fubmitted to the
" ftamp act without actual oppofition ; but,
" the Virginia refolutions proved the alarum
" bell. From that time libels of the moft
" atrocious kind have fwarmed and been
" urged with fo much vehemence, and fo
" induftrioufly repeated, that I have confi-
" dered them as preludes to action ; but I
" did not think that it would have com-
" menced fo early, or been carried to fuch
" lengths as it has been." And the letter
contains an account of " fifty gentlemen,
" actors in a riot, befides a much larger
" number behind the curtain," and adds
" the common talk is that the ftamp-act
" fhall not be executed here, that all the
" power of Great Britain fhall not oblige
" them to fubmit to it, and that they will
" die upon the place. In truth it will
" be impoffible to carry the ftamp act into
" execution untill frefh *powers* come from
" England." And in a fubfequent letter of
the fame month " it is my opinion that the
" worft that can happen fhould be expected
" and provided againft." p. 53 " The refo-
" lutions of Maffachufet's Bay were fimilar
" to thofe of Virginia. The board of trade
" reprefented, that the abettors and perpe-
" trators of the difturbances in Auguft, in
                                " America,

" America, declare a general refolution to
" oppofe and prevent the execution of the
" act, and that the magiftracy there, was
" utterly incapable of refifting or fuppreffing
" thefe tumults and diforders. The Provi-
" dence Gazette extraordinary, of the 14th
" of the fame month fays, that his Majefty's
" liege people, the inhabitants of America,
" are not bound to yield obedience to any
" *internal* taxation other than of the Gene-
" neral affembly." P. 60 " The intelligence
" from other hands and other quarters is
" all of the fame kind," and p. 63 confef-
fes, that " the moft alarming informations
" had been received fo long ago as the 27th
" of July," and afterwards, " the plan of a
" general affembly of committees, which
" had proceeded from *Maffachufet's Bay*,
" difcovered more of a regular fyftem of re-
" fiftance." P. 68 takes notice of a letter
dated in September reprefenting, " that there
" was *a general fcheme concerted throughout*
" *America;*" and afterwards another letter
dated in the fame month informs, " that
" they grew more and more inflamed, and
" declared they would not fubmit to the
" ftamp act upon any account, or in any
" inftance," and another in that month
fays, " many declare they will ward off the
" ftamp act, untill they can get *France*
" or *Spain* to protect them." The pamphlet likewife afferts, that " the fchemes of
" independance were formed and guided by
" the lawyers and fupported by the princi-
" pals

" pals of the provinces." And p. 97 ſpeaks
of their " raiſing a regular body of forces
" to be oppoſed to thoſe of England; that
" the principal men of different parties,
" were reconciled to each other; and, that
" the militia refuſed to obey the Captain
" General."

After reading theſe faithful extracts
from the ſtamp authors own notes, any body
may I think ſay, " out of thy own mouth
" will I judge thee, wicked ſcribbler." And
it is impoſſible that either you, or the officers in America could upon ſuch evidence
think that the act would be obeyed. For
the moment that it arrived, the province
of Virginia came to thoſe reſolutions which
were an alarum bell to the whole continent,
and every province abetted the ſame principles, and it was manifeſt to the governors,
that theſe were not mere verbal aſſertions,
but principles of action; ſo that thoſe who
had never before ſeen the leaſt inclination
in the inhabitants of America, to diſpute
by force with England, and had therefore
haſtily written over, that they made no
doubt but the act would be obeyed, ſoon
changed their tone and confeſſed their miſ-
take. In ſhort, the people were to a man
determined to reſiſt, and the whole train of
evidence proves it; their warm remonſtrances
againſt the act to our own legiſlature, the
reſolutions of their aſſemblies, their news
papers, which the governors dared not to
proſecute; their riots, headed by the moſt
ſubſtantial

fubftantial men among them, the active part taken by the body of lawyers, the reconciliation of all parties, the general union and communication of the feveral provinces on that continent, which before could never be brought to agree together in any one thing; the refufal of the militia and provincial forces to obey the orders of our Governors, or even of our Captain General, and finally their taking meafures to fecure fome of the towns and to raife forces. Thefe are a cloud of witneffes to one and the fame point, which muft carry full evidence of the thing to every man.

Nay it is my opinion that the framer of the ftamp act forefaw it would be oppofed and not obeyed, by his laying a ftamp upon the clearances of fhips outwards, which is not the cafe here and which was impofed there, merely to force down the act under the penalty of ftopping the whole trade of the country. There is no other reafon to be affigned for fuch an impofition. And this I fuppofe is one of the grounds for the ftamp writers glorying, that " the ftamp " act was formed to *execute* itfelf." But if I agree with him herein, it muft be by taking the word in a different fenfe from this politician, and then it may be true, that this act was calculated to be its own executioner, and to have a chance likewife for giving a finifhing ftroke to the *execution* of all our other laws and government there; had not the madnefs of the furious miniftry

try that planned it, done their own bufinefs
here firft, by endeavouring for the fake of
riveting their power to fcrew tighter than
need be in a ticklifh point at home, and
fo (to ufe his own phrafe) *executed* themfelves when they leaft intended it, very much
to the fatisfaction of the whole nation.
I think I may fay any wife man fpeculating
upon the fubject would originally have feen
the probability there was from the nature
of the thing, coupled with the actual circumftances of the colonies, that the act
would be oppofed; efpecially as many of
the inhabitants were of a very fturdy race,
who had fled thither from the tyrannies of
Charles I. and Oliver Cromwell, for the
fole purpofe of enjoying liberty and property. And therefore it is marvellous that
the planner of the tax did not provide means
adequate to the occafion for enforcing obedience to it. But it is plain from his
own evidence that no provifion of this fort
was made. For, " the *Commander in chief*
" fays the forces are greatly fcattered and
" divided over that *vaft* continent, and that
" a junction might be prevented by froft."
Now furely a circumfpect man who had
undertaken a hazardous and precarious thing
would have taken alfo every precaution
for not being defeated and difappointed.
But a total infatuation feems to have attended the projector from the beginning to
the end. Now there having been no provifion made for enforcing this act, what excufe

cuſe can a miniſter have, who, for the ſake
of going a new way to work, in the
raiſing of ſuch a ſmall ſum as 70,000*l.* a
year, would riſque a civil war; for let the
event be ever ſo ſure of our ſide, the Colonies muſt be ſo impoveriſhed and undone
by it, that they would probably be rendered
unable to pay the tax in queſtion and be
likewiſe ſo much the leſs capable for the
future of taking off the manufactures that
we have hitherto ſupplied them with. To
ſay nothing of the great additional expence
we muſt be at in any war with them, which
would alone countervail the whole amount
of ſuch a tax. Indeed, the refuſal to let
them raiſe their own money themſelves, or
(as the New York reſolution words it)
" for the *people of Great Britain,* to grant to
" his Majeſty the property of *the people there,*
" would be unreaſonable and render uſeleſs
" their legiſlation." Nothing ſeems to me
to excuſe ſuch a proceeding, but the Colonies
having abſolutely refuſed (when reaſonably
required) in their own aſſemblies, to give any
ſupplies, towards defraying the expence
that Great Britain has been at, upon their
account ; or elſe a reſiſtance of any of our
acts, impoſing duties upon their exports
or imports, or a denial to conform to our
regulations, touching their manufactures.
At the ſame time I muſt allow, that even
whilſt bills for theſe latter purpoſes are de-
pending in parliament, I think they ſhould
be heard by their agents and council at the

L   bar,

bar, fo that nothing fhould be done to affect their interefts without their having an
opportunity, at leaft of fhewing every objection, hardfhip, inequality, or injuftice
that might attend it. And when this is
done, our interefts and theirs, are fo reciprocal and interwoven, that nothing unjuft
can ever be done to them, becaufe there is
nothing that can be eventually good for one
country which will be detrimental to the
other. Whereas, there is not only the appearance of great tyranny in laying reftraints
upon people, without hearing what they
have to fay againft it, but in all probability
what is completely right will hardly ever
be compaffed without it.

As the fupreme government of fovereignty
of Great Britain, lies in the King, Lords,
and Commons ; fo every conqueft made by
Britifh force, all acquifitions by treaty, and
every colony fent out from hence, muft belong to this fupreme government, and for
this reafon, the King cannot govern the Colonies independent of his Britifh parliament,
he making but a part of the Britifh fovereignty, and therefore it is, that the controll over the whole Britifh empire lies, with
the King, Lords, and Commons, as the
fovereign of the whole. But this controll
fhould be exercifed with due regard to all
privileges, laws, and judicatures ; in fhort, it
it is a prefumptuous, as well as unpopular
thing, to depart from the antient forms of a
ftate, and to go out of the ufual road of
government;

government; and, without abſolute neceſſity, ſhould never be done, becauſe it may be dangerous, and will, in all probability, be attended with much inconvenience, if not injuſtice.

I have no doubt but that we could ſubdue our colonies, even if France and Spain were to abet them ; and, by the bye, ſome of the Americans intimated they would even go there for aid, rather than ſubmit to the ſtamp act. But ſuch a victory, I ſhould nevertheleſs think the moſt undeſirable we could have. And, God forbid, that, like the ſtamp author, I ſhould, by ill uſage, drive the plantations into a revolt, in order to have the glory of triumphing over them afterwards. It is our intereſt ſurely that they ſhould flouriſh and increaſe; and as there is all the reaſon in the world that they ſhould contribute to the general expence of the ſtate, ſo I queſtion not but they will ever be ready to do ſo; but then let them find out their own taxes, and raiſe their own money in their own way. They have had the privilege of doing ſo hitherto, and I am deſirous of their continuing to enjoy it.

It makes my blood run cold, when I ſee the pamphleteer endeavouring to whet us againſt the Americans, and to put us upon drawing the ſword, for the ſake of enforcing the ſtamp act, although obliged at the ſame time to confeſs, that " many trading towns " in Great Britain, and principal merchants
" in

" in London, did affift the Americans, to
" accomplifh the ends of the miniftry" in
getting it repealed. So that, he would
prompt us to make war upon our colonies,
for the purpofe of carrying into execution
an odious law, that Great Britain, as well
as all America, have complained of. And
yet next to the folly of the tax, would be,
I think, the engaging in a war for its defence. But, What a ftrange and obftinate
temper muft that be, which neither humanity, nor the voice of mankind can affect!
after " blaming the minifter for not fending
" an augmentation of force," he proceeds
to tell us, that " a body of five thoufand
" men, might have been formed, ready and
" able to reduce the revolting provinces to
" obedience," and then labours through
three hundred pages, to depreciate an a-
miable and gallant officer, now high in the
civil department for tamenefs and want of
fpirit on this account. And yet he knows
that the General was among the foremoft
who difapproved the meafure originally, declared he would take the firft opportunity
of endeavouring its repeal, and has fince
actually bore an eminent part in that falutary
ftep. In fact, all the fucceeding miniftry,
the merchants in general, and the bulk of
the kingdom, including even a majority of
the ill fated ftamp-authors friends, were
convinced at laft of the imprudence, hardfhip, and injuftice of the act, and therefore
wifhed for the return of the feffion of parliament

liament to fet about the getting rid of it.
Infomuch that there was fcarcely a man,
befides the inflexible framer of it, but confeffed it would be right, in point of policy,
whether the act were conftitutional or not,
to refcind it; indeed fome few were for
retaining the impofition upon cards and dice,
by way of evidencing our right to lay the
tax, but not for the fake of the revenue
from thence. Nay then, fays the great minifter *now* in confidence with his majefty,
feeing the Americans complain of your laying
an internal tax upon them, in which I
think they have reafon, having a primary
right to do it themfelves, and, till they refufe fo to do, it is unjuft for us to inter-
fere; if you agree to give up the fubftance,
let us not quarrel about the fhadow; if you
part with the whole benefit do not leave the
fting behind. The repeal fhould be gracious
and complete.

When it was refolved therefore, by nine
parts in ten of our minifters and legiflators,
to give up the tax and to repeal the act
laying it; how ftrange, how mad would
it have been to do what this obftinate author, fays we ought to have done? for,
would any nation imbrue its hands in the
blood of a colony, unneceffarily and for no
purpofe, but that of compelling obedience
to a ftatute, which every body held to be im-
politic, and the new miniftry wifhed to an-
nul and bury in oblivion? in fuch cafe
would any wife man put the ftrongeft, the
worft

worſt conſtruction, upon every libellous
ſpeech, warm vote, or riotous proceeding
of the ſufferers, in order to found a
pretence for putting them to the ſword?
would not a diſpaſſionate and true patriot
to overlook the wiſh as much as might be, intemperance
of fellow ſubjects, upon ſuch an occaſion?
let ſatisfaction be made to the private perſons injured, by thoſe who have commit-
ted the outrage, or by the province where
it happened; but let not the heavy hand
of this ſtate cruſh them, let not the
armies and navies of the mother country
revenge with a ſevere and vindictive ſpirit,
every inſult offered to its government by
froward daughter colonies, that if
their rights have been invaded, ſome change
ſhould be paſſed over, and
made, which no time
Inhabitants will increaſe, and trade flouriſh,
where lenity is experienced and faults for-
given, but harſh treatment and rigorous
juſtice, eſpecially in new caſes, where rights
are made a queſtion, will prevent popu-
lation, damp the ſpirit of induſtry, and
deſtroy the ends of colonization. It was
therefore, in my humble opinion, a moſt
fortunate event for the whole Britiſh ſtate,
that our Royal Maſter called other gentlemen into his ſervice, and particularly
Mr. C——, whoſe conciliating behaviour
ſoon allayed thoſe animoſities, which ill-
timed ſeverity would have quickly ſharpened
into open rebellion, the conſequence of
which

which would have been such military proceedings, as I hope never to see any occasion
for. At the same time, this calm conduct in
a man of much real corrage, so often proved
in fields of battle, is more meritorious than
it would have been in a mere civil officer.
The uniform, firm, but humane demeanor
of this gentleman, which was equally shewn
to all the provinces, and has answered so well,
is ridiculed by the writer to the stamp act,
as so much warm water, prescribed by way
of general potion for every disorder. On
the contrary forsooth, he wanted to have
had nothing but hot water made use of;
now, as I never wish to see our colonies put
into such, I am very glad they were taken
from under his management, left both they
and ourselves should have been intirely
scalded by this miserable physician.

In short. Mr. Secretary *Conway's* prudent
procedure has at length restored health and
a sound constitution to that continent where
the Stamp Master had well nigh raised a general inflammation that would at least have
endangered the destruction of the whole.
It is to me wonderful that the stamp author
should opiniater this matter so long, and
should persist against the sense of mankind
in declaring " the success and good effect
" of the act would have still encreased the
" reputation of the minister who planned
" it," and should aim at being humorous on
Mr. *Conway's* expostulary directions for being *Essays on Obedience*, and *Dissertations on
Prudence*

Prudence and Levity. Indeed, he laughs at
the Secretary for kindly " fuppofing that
" the refiftance can only have found place
" among the lower and more ignorant of
" the people," and for faying, " he would
" fooner cut off his right hand than order
" troops to march to fupprefs a claim of
" freedom;" and then adds, that " this
" conduct has loft to Great Britain the
" hands of all the inhabitants of America."
Whereas, I believe, there is not a fober
man who does not think the very reverfe,
and that if this outrageous Stamp Author
would really (which I doubt) have crammed
his act down the throats of the Americans,
had he continued minifter, he would, by
fucceeding in that point, have rendered them
no longer advantageous to this country, as
their fubjection muft have been brought
about and maintained by much expence, and
every thing there, inftead of flourifhing,
would have drooped and languifhed for the
time to come. It does not furprife me to
fee him openly bantering any minifter for
paying a regard to *claims of freedom,* and for
being unwilling *to fupprefs them by troops*;
the beginning of this long letter will inform the reader why; nor am I at all dif-
pleafed with him for being fo felf-fatisfied
as to think himfelf wifer than all the
world befides. His principles of government, and his abilities for miniftry have
been fo thoroughly experienced, that I believe they will never more do much hurt;
and

and therefore he may vaunt them as much as he pleafes, and proclaim himfelf whenever he can, to be the only clever fellow in the realm. It is not his vanity and felf-fufficiency, but his adminiftration that I beg leave to object to. Indeed, fo fully perfuaded am I, that the late financier would have done irreparable mifchief to England, by inforcing his tax in America; that I fear as it is, he may have layed the foundation for diftruft, grudge and ill-will there, and thus been the occafion already of their drawing fewer manufactures from hence than ufual, and of their contriving more methods of doing without them for the future. His intention, I dare fay, was originally good, but his head is fo unequal to large confiderations of this fort, and his obftinacy fo great in not receding from any thing he has once projected, that I look upon him as wholly unfit for the fuperior provinces of finance, altho' he may make a very ufeful and induftrious drudge in fome of the fubordinate departments. Moreover a man that nothing will convince of his errors, is never likely to mend, for he never fees things in the right light; and this feems to be particularly the cafe with the ftamp author, who, fo far from feeing that the real objectionablenefs of the tax had united both the Colonies and the Englifh merchants in calling out for its repeal, imagines it was folely brought about by political intrigue of the Great Commoner, it

M   being

being his " intereft that all the capital
" meafures of the former miniftry fhould
" be thought wrong." And he then finds
occafion to fay, " Mr. *Grenville* retained
" the ufelefs and exploded idea of a com-
" mon weal and public intereft, purfuing a
" plan of *Englifh* policy abroad, and of
" œconomy and improvement *at home; while*
" Mr. *Pitt* acquired popularity by adopting
" the moft expenfive *German* meafures, and
" impofing the moft fevere taxes to fupport
" them." Now, I will not deny that Mr.
Grenville did purfue a plan of œconomy and
improvement at home, for it is faid he is
very rich and has otherwife greatly improv-
ed his circumftances by procuring a teller-
fhip for his infant fon, of all which, no
doubt his family will reap the benefit. And
I am inclined to think, upon reviewing what
I have fuggefted in the foregoing part of
this work, that the idea which he has retained of a common weal, public intereft,
and Englifh policy is ufelefs, and therefore
not improperly exploded ; becaufe we have
long ceafed to think that he is a good
legiflator, whofe acts muft in the one part
be carried into execution by difpenfing
treafury orders, and in the other by the
fword, or elfe muft remain unexecuted at
all, as was the cafe with the ftamp act. But
I can agree no farther with this gentleman ;
and indeed I fancy he has by miftake printed
while for *after he and,* becaufe it is certain
that *whilft* Mr. *Pitt* was acquiring popularity

larity by German meafures and impofing taxes to fupport them, Mr. *Grenville*, who was then high in office, poffeffed of a very lucrative employ, and a member of the Privy Council, concurred both there and in Parliament with Mr. *Pitt*, as well about the meafures as the taxes. Nay, in truth no-body oppofed either, infomuch that there was an unanimity in parliament during that period never known before or fince. And it was not till the making of the laft peace that Mr. *Pitt* left adminiftration, when Mr. *Grenville* concurred with *Lord Bute* in that and the cyder tax and the fubfequent mea-fures. Indeed, as to the late tax upon A-merica, which fet all the colonies againft Great Britain, it is faid, I know, by his friends to have been wholly his.

But, our author now betakes himfelf to his favourite employment the making a long harangue, even without any audience, and fays, " If the public fee with regret the " power of government in the hands of " Lord C—, it is from the dread not fo " much of his continental as of his colonial " fyftem ; it was from the commerce of the " American part of our dominions that " thofe refources were to be drawn, which " his extravagance have rendered fo necef-" fary, who is almoft the only man in Eng-" land who ventures to affert that it owes " us no fubjeſtion and profeffes on princi-" ples to throw them from us."

Enough

Enough has been said to shew how far we
are obliged to the stamp author for *his*
colonial system with respect to its advanta-
geousness, and therefore I shall not take
any particular notice of what is here flung
out again upon that subject, but attend to
the latter part of the paragraph. Whereon I shall singly remark that a writer must
either be deficient in sense or honesty who
can think there is any truth in it. It has
been before observed that a denial of our
right to lay any internal tax in America,
without first applying to their several assem-
blies for the purpose, does not imply that
we have no right to bind it immediately by
other laws, or that we mean to throw it off
from us. For does any man deny that Ire-
land is subject to us, although she has and
does exercise, and every body allows her the
right of internally taxing herself. The
great statesman here alluded to, is only for
carrying on government every where in the
usual, constitutional channel, without in-
fringing or violating the rights and fran-
chises of any part of the British subjects.
It has been his merit and lot to subdue our
foreign enemies, and to protect our domestic
civil rights, when his opposers were for
submitting to the former, and tyrannizing
over the latter. And I trust, his Majesty
will find that his conduct has not only rendered his reign glorious abroad, but more
respectable at home. His colonies are no
longer at variance with their mother country,

try, but ready to affift her when required
fo to do. They are neither thrown off nor
defirous of being fo, and they know very
well that " fupport is due in return for pro-
" tection" *in liberty and property* ; wherefore
their affemblies will always for the future,
with chearfulnefs contribute accordingly.

Before I conclude I muft take notice of
p. 131. where the inconfiderate writer to
the ftamp act fays, " It would be unjuft
" to reproach the miniftry with the effemi-
" nate, uncertain and even ungrammatical
" expreffions in which they clothe the fen-
" timents which they attribute to their fo-
" vereign, becaufe it is probable they ufed
" on this occafion the beft expreffions in
" their power." For if I recollect right
fome worthy minifters not long ago expell-
ed from parliament, profecuted and out-
lawed Mr. *Wilkes* for faying in print that
the *miniftry had made his Majefty affert a falfity.*
Now, if this were the punifhment inflicted
by that miniftry, the ftamp author fhould
not tell the world that the fucceeding miniftry had made his majefty exprefs himfelf
effeminately, uncertainly and *ungrammattically,*
feeing the excufe of its being purely intended as an infult upon the minifter and not
upon his fovereign has been held infuffi-
cient, and the author ruined for what he
faid. Now, it is pretty difficult to deter-
mine which of the two is the moft con-
temptuous libel ; therefore what could the
ftamp author, fhould he even be a member,

urge

urge againſt parliamentary expulſion, and
againſt pillory, fine and impriſonment by
the *King's Bench*, which might all too be
going on at the ſame time, as no *privilege*,
you know, lies in the caſe ?

I have now done with this candid, con-
ſiſtent and able *pleader* for what he calls (by
a figure of ſpeech) *the cauſe of Great Britain*,
that is, for the ſtamp act ; but I ought not
to bid him a final farewell without teſtify-
ing in ſober earneſt, my real commenda-
tion of the caution he has ſhewn in leaving
chaſms to prevent the writers of the letters
he has cited from *being diſcovered*. Becauſe
I can eaſily believe his *American correſpon-*
dent, when he *ſays* " I communicate things
" at the riſque of my life," and for my own
part I wiſh from the ſame principle of common humanity that a certain proteſt had
not held forth Governor *Bernard* by name
to the reſentment and indignation of an
exaſperated province. It was not neceſſary
to the argument, and might be fatal to the
governor ; and in my opinion too, it would
not diſcredit even the nobleſt of perſons to
ſhew ſome regard in party diſputes to the
life of an excellent man, whilſt they are
availing themſelves of his teſtimony. It is
plain however, let whiſper intimate what it
will, that the ſtamp author could have no
hand in writing or printing this proteſt, for
if he had there would have been *a chaſm left*
in that part, at leaſt. It was alſo peculiar-
ly unfortunate for Mr. *Bernard* that the im-
preſſion

preffion of this proteft fhould have been very quickly made and moft induftrioufly circulated as well as publicly fold, becaufe all the Americans and their agents had an opportunity thereby of immediately difperfing copies over the whole continent of America, where he then was. I lament the matter the more, by reafon this able governor acted the moft meritorious of all parts : in earneftly trying in the firft place to diffuade our minifters from laying the tax, by many very urgent arguments ; and afterwards when it was layed, by endeavouring as ftrenuoufly to make the people there fubmit to it as a law, and attempt only to get it repealed by remonftrance, and not by riot and refiftance, left Great Britain fhould be fo offended as to proceed againft them by force, and fubdue them as rebels, inftead of regarding them as fuffering fubjects entitled to relief. In fhort, his conduct was fuch as fhould procure him lafting honor in both countries. For, in his fituation he could not avoid giving true intelligence of what was paffing, with his judgment of what was neceffary in either event for our government to do ; and confidering the provocations he daily met with upon the fpot, it is amazing that he fhould be fo little animated with refentment in the fequel, very few men would have acted fo humanely, fo difcreetly, fo moderately, and withal fo confiftently and fo firmly. But, notwithftanding all this, any Englifhman muft be difliked there in fuch a ferment and

commotion,

commotion, who did his duty as a governor, and let his fovereign know the true ftate of things. The naming him, therefore in the proteft, I cannot reconcile with humanity or political prudence.

This is all I fhall fay to you, G——, upon the ftamp act, and think you had better have done with it too; for like fome other matters of bad odor, the more it is ftirred the more noifome it will become. However, I fhould not let you depart without reminding you that the Great commoner, whom you have fo much traduced, always faid to every body who came near him at the time, that all the plan talked of with regard to America was wrong, the nature of the tax, and the mode of laying it, and the jurifdiction for enforcing it; and that nothing but gout prevented his oppofing the whole of it in parliament. You heard of this frequently, and therefore you fhould not let your penman have infinuated the contrary; as if no man declared againft the meafure whilft it was tranfacting, or then doubted about the right or the expediency of the meafure.

You know alfo that the fame difcourfe was held by the particular and avowed friend of this illuftrious perfonage, I mean by the great lawyer who was then fo much diftinguifhed by the people, and has fince been ennobled by the crown, for being the faithful affertor of lawful Englifh liberty. This could not be done by him, it is true, in parliament,

liament, being no member, but his senti-
ments were as certainly known to you as the
contents of the American petitions that were
not received there. You plume yourself,
therefore, very improperly upon " no one
" person having been then found, *in either*
" *house*, who would declare it to be his opi-
" nion that America was not in this instance
" to be *subject* to Great Britain," as you
chuse, after all, most unwarrantably to phrase
it. The popularity which the Great Commoner once had, and which you suppose he
has now lost by being a peer, will never be
extinguished, by maintaining that all British
subjects should be represented in some way
or other in order to be taxed, or by going
from the one house of parliament into the
other; unless his principles of government
should be found to vary with his place ; but,
I presume both he and his great legal friend
will shew this nation with respect to these
their local changes *Cælum non animum mu-
tant*, as most certainly the English settled in
America have shewn that those do not—*qui
trans mare currunt*. Therefore G——, do
not let places and titles engross your attention, but look at measures and things, and
when you find these ill-judged and arbitra-
rily pursued, withstand, oppose, attack, pro-
secute, impeach the authors as wrong-
headed, violent men, and I will join even
you in the cause. For to tell you the truth,
I think the public should be very attentive
to what is done, and very inattentive to the

N   actors.

actors. It matters not the nation whether
this or that proud connection be offended by
some little alteration in the post or profit of
a friend, let ever so much private worth be
thrown into the scale ; and much less whether any great man will turn his back on a
ministry, unless they engage to provide for
his necessitous retinue. Every good man
would undoubtedly wish that no such thing
as faction, party or connexion subsisted at
all, and that the worthiest of every denomi-
nation and inclining could be promoted,
whether opulent or needy ; but as political
associations and cabals will not permit this,
the public has great reason to be content
when such measures are pursued as make for
the general weal. Individuals must always
take the consequence of their personal at-
tachments ; the state as such has no concern
in the matter.

It is the common notion that our extraordinary minister whilst in office has been always inaccessible to mere visitors of whatever quality, and could never be talked with
about places, nor seen on any private
affairs ; but that he was open at all times to
any body of any condition, who had public
business to transact or to speak about, and
that he was upon these occasions the easiest
and most agreeable man in the world to
confer with. Now I cannot for my own
part blame a real statesman for such reserve,
or if you will distance, with respect to the
mere men of fashion and birth, who neither
think

think nor care about the ſtate, nor have any
thing but their own particular points to ſo-
licit. This being the caſe, I was ſurpriſed
the other day to hear a very ingenious gentleman of a neighbouring iſland talk of the
miniſter as utterly inapproachable, excepting
by choſen ſpirits, and that theſe could only
approach him with their ſupplications, co-
vering their faces, like the angels of *Milton*
who hide themſelves with their wings before
the deity. I enquired therefore ſeriouſly
into the faƈt, and learned there was no
foundation for it; and that probably it was
no more than a ſublime idea of a beautiful
imagination. But I am rather, I confeſs,
apt to ſuſpeƈt myſelf that it may really have
been the ſingular effeƈt of that particular
awe and reverence which a baſhful man always feels within himſelf, when he appears
before the great, and may in this inſtance
perhaps be only the genuine offspring of that
native ſhamefacedneſs ſo very remarkable in
this diffident young politician, heightened
withal by the natural and innate modeſty of
the country from whence he comes. However, the ſources of human error are ſo va-
rious, that I don't care to be poſitive in matters of this difficulty, and therefore I merely
ſubmit my opinion to your greater expe-
rience.

Before I fold up my letter, pray let me
aſk one queſtion concerning the Eaſt India
affairs. As you have *always of late* been ſo
full of complaints about the ſize of the national

tional debt, I take it for granted what the world reports cannot be true. The rumor is that you are averfe to the public's gaining any revenue from all the territories there that our people have taken hold of; nay, to the feeing whether the public that protected the company during the laft war is not fo far interefted as to have a right to be apprized of the nature of the acquifitions. Now fuch a bruit aftonifhes me. For, if I underftand right, this great company have traded exceedingly beyond their charter, and have likewife made the conqueft of a vaft rich and populous region; in either of which cafes the ftate at large has a right to avail themfelves of the event. Monopolies are to be carried no farther than the purpofes of trade required; therefore the parliament, as the great inquifition of the nation fhould inquire into their proceedings, as they did fome years ago into thofe of the *Hudfons Bay* company, and fee whether any thing and what is proper to be done thereon, and give fuch advice upon the whole to the crown as they fhall fee fit. Indeed, as fuch a tract of territory is acquired, it behoves the public to look after it. It is certain that no Englifhman can acquire any lands or territorial poffeffions by conqueft, and hold them independant of the crown for their own benefit, for all fuch acquifitions will belong to the ftate, according to every writer upon thefe matters. Now, the common report is, that this thriving company,

in

in confequence of many victories, and the
dread of their arms, got poffeffion of the
immenfe tract in queftion, and then took a
ceffion or grant of the whole revenue, force
and ufufruct thereof from a perfon whom
they fet up for the purpofe as Emperor or
Mogul, in confideration of a fmall ftipend
to be paid him. This emperor forfooth,
being neither in poffeffion of any dominions, nor having any more power or capacity
of making refiftance, or of denying them
what they afked, or of refuming it again if
the ftipend was not payed, than myfelf.
Now, do you think, or would you allow,
that a grant to the Americans from the Pretender to hold of him in chief, paying
300l. a year, in lieu of all taxes and duties
whatever to Great Britain, would be deemed
a fufficient bar to parliaments interfering
there? In fhort, the company have the
entire command of the country ceded; its
forces and revenues, and can do with the
fame whatever they pleafe. And then the
queftion is, whether this fhall be confidered as a mercantile purchafe or acqueft by
mutual bargain and reciprocal treaty, or the
fruit of arms and of terms impofed by
conquerors through the terror of military
force, and coertion over a naked and defencelefs poffeffor and inhabitants. And
though the determination be not difficult,
I fhall fay nothing to it. Be it as it may, it
is beyond a doubt that the parliament have
a right to enquire, and the public to expect
they

they fhould, into the conduct of fuch a pro-
digious monopoly as this, when whole provinces and extenfive territories are obtained,
and military expeditions carried on, which
are not the ordinary means of commerce,
or the bufinefs and concern of a trading
company. Regions and wealth fo acquired,
by the fword, cannot be deemed the profits
of traffic. In a word, the competency of a
parliamentary inquiry, and the propriety of
one, in fuch circumftances and where the
object is of fo much importance to the trade
and fhipping of the Britannic empire, cannot be denied. Every man is interefted in
it, and no friend to his country can opp
it. When the proceedings of   7
in India are fully underftoo.   .-
ed, if any private rights come   ir
queftions on the legal import c   a
charter arife, it will be very ea.; for parliament to advife and direct their being argued
and decided in the proper jurifdictions.
God forbid that the private right or property of any individual, or any acquifitions
of the company as a trading company fhould
be invaded, much lefs taken from them.
But if the revenues of this newly acquired
dominion rightfully belong to the public
and can be applied to the eafing our national
debt, will it not, G——, be an excellent
thing ? Is it not therefore, a great idea and
a proper object for parliamentary examina-
tion ? The inquiry will injure no private
rights, nor deprive the company of any
privileges

privileges they are intitled to by charter;
but since they are British subjects, engage in
wars, fight battles, make conquests and
then treaties, and have the wealth of all
the Indies almost at command, it is time
surely for the government to which they
belong to be informed of the nature of their
proceedings. It seems to me to be as clear
a case for the interposition of parliament as
ever occurred in the course of time. And
nothing but the envy of a luckless exploded
financier, aided by jobbers and the *Jonathans*
of the day could stir any opposition to so
great and so promising an inquiry. The
political opposers of the measure can only
be afraid that too much glory will redound
to the author of it; and the others that the
profits of their gaming will be less ; both
being fully confident that great national benefit will and must be the consequence. Unhappy baneful spirits ! The very directors
and old proprietors of E. I. stock, desire
the inquiry, knowing the affairs to be become of too great magnitude to be managed
or preserved now, without the eye and hand
of government itself. However a man who
has once taken the part of opposing any inquiry as unjust and been beaten off it, can
never afterwards be guilty of an equal ab-
surdity; unless by shifting directly about,
upon a notion that the government and the
company are making a bargain, and thereupon declaring that he thinks in such case
the *parliament* ought *publickly* to inspect most
minutely

minutely their commerical affairs, and examine even into all their private debts and
credits, as particularly as a fraudulent
bankrupt's concerns are vifited by his com-
miffioners. At leaft fuch rare contrariety
and beautiful variegated conduct will never
be believed poffible, until actually put in
practice, even in political life. Wherefore
my laft words to *you* G——, fhall be, as you
tender your own reputation with the Commons of England at large, proceed no further, leaft the public fhould think that their
good and you muft be for ever incompatible.
To the dereliction of the Manila ranfom, the
exclufion of Spanifh bullion, and the difregard of Portugal gold, do not add a re-
jection, and poffibly the total lofs of the
wealth of the Indies, but let this laft for the
fake of your country, and in fpite of faction,
be at leaft a national care. *Sat famæ vixifti.*

I am, &c.

Richmond,
Jan. 18, 1767.

L.

F I N I S.